# The Tree Care Primer

By
Christopher Roddick with Beth Hanson

Sigrun Wolff Saphire
SENIOR EDITOR

Janet Marinelli
CONSULTING EDITOR

Mark Tebbitt
SCIENCE EDITOR

Elizabeth Ennis
ART DIRECTOR

Joni Blackburn
COPY EDITOR

Elizabeth Peters
DIRECTOR OF
PUBLICATIONS

Steven Clemants
VICE-PRESIDENT,
SCIENCE &
PUBLICATIONS

Scot Medbury
PRESIDENT

Elizabeth Scholtz
DIRECTOR
EMERITUS

Handbook #186

Copyright © 2007 by Brooklyn Botanic Garden, Inc.

*All-Region Guides*, formerly *21st-Century Gardening Series*, are published three times a year at 1000 Washington Ave., Brooklyn, NY 11225.

Subscription included in Brooklyn Botanic Garden subscriber membership dues ($35 per year; $45 outside the United States).

ISBN 13: 978-1-889538-29-7
ISBN 10: 1-889538-29-9

Printed by Cadmus Communications.
Printed on recycled paper.

**Above: The light, moisture, and soil conditions found in natural forest habitats are often strikingly different from the environments we give trees in suburban yards and city streets.**

**Cover: When growing conditions are right, trees such as this oak can live for hundreds of years.**

# The Tree Care Primer

# Getting to Know Trees

What do you see when you look at a tree? Chances are you are only a short walk away from one right now, even if you live in a big city, so go find one and take a look. At first glance, there are a trunk, branches, leaves, perhaps even flowers or fruits such as nuts or cherries. But what else can you tell about the tree—how is its health? How old is it? How has it been cared for? If you are fortunate enough to have trees in your yard or garden, it pays to know about them in order to keep them—and you—happy.

First of all, if you don't know a tree, try to identify it noting a few general features. What type is it—deciduous or evergreen? What do the leaves look like? The bark? Does it have fruit? What is its form, or overall growth pattern—pyramidal, spreading, columnar, or layered, etc.? Refer to a field guide or tree-identification site on the Internet (see "For More Information," page 114) to find out what you're looking at.

When I look at a tree, the first thing I do as an arborist is determine its life stage: Is it juvenile, mature, or ancient? I look at its size, shape, and branching pattern, and I examine the bark to learn its pruning history. I make note of many other characteristics that allow me to piece together information about the tree's life stage and history. I can do this because a tree's architecture forms an accurate record of its past and gives each tree its own unique character—for better or worse. That's because trees undergo dynamic changes all their lives as they respond to the pressures in the world around them.

In a man-made landscape, trees must respond to conditions that can be far more challenging than anything nature has to offer. We transplant trees, sometimes in completely unsuitable places, drastically prune them, and try to grow lawns under them. Street and urban trees face some of the toughest tests: road salt, limited space for roots and branches, compacted soils, and harsh reflected light and heat.

**Beyond the attention-grabbing bright autumn fruits, this crabapple (*Malus* cultivar) reveals much about its life story in its architecture—to anyone willing to take a closer look.**

Despite all the challenges that trees encounter there is much you can do to make life easier for them, as you will find out in this book. You'll learn how to determine which trees may be suitable for a particular spot. Then you find out how to select the healthiest trees at a nursery and get them started right by planting properly. You will find detailed guidance for the best pruning practices for juvenile, mature, and veteran trees; and learn how proper watering, mulching, and pruning help keep trees healthy. You'll also find out how to recognize hazardous conditions and the best ways to prevent or remedy them. There's even a chapter on dying and dead trees that explains the important roles they play as habitat for wildlife. To help you with terms for tree anatomy and functions, there's a glossary on page 109.

Just as a good doctor cares for each patient a little differently depending on the patient's age, condition, and medical history, so should we treat our trees. By understanding the growth and survival strategies of various tree species and their specific structural development or architecture, you will be better prepared to care for all your trees at each of their life stages.

# From Tree Growth to Tree Care

Trees can grow larger than any other plant because they are able to make wood to support their mass. This, however, requires them to photosynthesize more and to produce more sugars and carbohydrates than other plants. As trees use a lot of energy to maintain their mass, creating a new flush of growth every year, they also contribute to the environment by producing sugars, binding up carbon dioxide from the air, and emitting oxygen, thereby making life possible—and pleasant—for organisms like us. (I once saw a billboard in California that said, "Trees give us oxygen, really good trees give us avocados.") Trees are also large suppliers in nature's decomposition cycle: As leaves and limbs fall and break down, their matter returns to the soil, supporting other organisms.

Like people, trees go through changes over the course of their lives as they develop from tiny seedlings to mature trees and eventually die, and just like people they are not simply products of their genes. Over a lifetime of responding to environmental pressures, each tree develops unique characteristics that define its architecture, or, one might say, its "personality." As it develops, a tree adjusts to its surroundings by optimizing growth—for example, by adding more wood to a weak area of the trunk, adding more roots on its windward side for stability, or by growing toward the light. It reacts to injury by producing chemicals that help fight off or stop the spread of infections through a process called compartmentalization (see "Defense," page 16). It economizes, using different strategies to maximize energy resources.

**Trees help make life on earth possible. Taken together, trees capture almost half of the .1 percent of the sun's energy photosynthesized by terrestrial organisms. Other major sun-trapping organisms are ocean algae, prairie grass, and tundra lichens.**

**Young trees like this oak seedling spend a lot of energy on growth "to get their heads above the crowd." Once they are mature, trees devote more resources to reproduction and defense.**

In addition to pressures occurring in the natural environment like competition for light and space from other trees, pest and disease outbreaks, storm damage, and droughts and floods, trees experience some stresses in a man-made landscape that are not found in nature and for which they are poorly equipped. A tree may be transplanted, possibly to a site ill-suited to its needs. Some of its limbs may be sawed off. The tree's root space may be disturbed by digging or harmed by the application of soil, turf, or pavement. In a sidewalk tree pit or other confined urban setting with lots of foot traffic, a tree may have to respond to even tougher challenges. It may experience seasonal showers of road salt or get regularly sprayed with dog urine. It may be confined to a very limited rooting space, have to contend with compacted soil, or be subjected to severe pruning when limbs get in the way of overhead utility lines. In brief, a tree's life is rarely easy, and it can be especially hard in an urban or suburban landscape that bears little resemblance to the natural landscape where trees evolved. The challenge for urban and suburban tree lovers is to give trees the best possible support in an often alien, if not outright hostile, environment.

## The Nature of Primary and Secondary Tree Growth

Good care starts with an understanding of how trees grow and function. Trees grow in two ways: by elongating at the tips and by adding girth. The two types of growth are respectively called primary growth and secondary growth. All growth occurs in the meristem, a group of undifferentiated cells that can divide to make specific new cells to create the various tissues and organs that form a tree. In other words, meristems are growing points. There are two major meristematic tissues in the stem: the buds and the cambium.

**Primary Growth** This type takes place at the ends of branches and roots. At the very tip of a twig is a bud called the terminal, or apical, bud, the point from which the stem elongates, producing new growth. The terminal bud produces the growth regulator substance called auxin, which suppresses growth from the lateral buds lined up along the stem behind it and is responsible for a type of growth called apical dominance. In trees with strong apical dominance, such as the tulip tree (*Lirodendron tulipifera*), pin oak (*Quercus palustris*), and pines (*Pinus* species), growth occurs mainly in the central leader. This results in a form that is very upright, called excurrent growth habit. Trees without strong apical dominance, such as elms (*Ulmus* species), crabapples (*Malus* species), and cherries (*Prunus* species), have spreading or vase-shaped crowns, or a decurrent growth habit.

The tree controls its own growth through the terminal bud. If the terminal bud is removed, either intentionally or by accident, the buds along the stem behind it are free to sprout without control. Think of the terminal bud as the "boss." If it is removed, the lateral buds position themselves to be the next boss. Gardeners take advantage of this growth pattern when they shear off terminal buds to create a hedge or pinch the tips off basil plants to create bushy growth. While this kind of pruning gives you a dense hedge and assures a bountiful basil harvest, it can be destructive for a tree. Understanding the role of the terminal bud is critical to successful tree pruning (see page 48).

**Trees continue growing all their lives, producing a new flush of growth each spring through the cambium or through terminal buds (right).**

These wood samples show secondary growth in different tree species. Each season trees add a new growth increment, or tree ring. The strong wooden support structure allows trees to be the tallest living organisms in the world.

Secondary Growth This growth enables trees to add girth every year. Between the inner bark and the wood of the tree lies a thin meristematic layer of cells, the cambium. In the cambium zone, new cells in the stem and roots are generated and divide, building new layers on the outside of the tree. The cambium produces vascular tissue called secondary phloem (inner bark) as its outer layer and secondary xylem (also known as wood) on the inside. Cambium also responds to the structural needs of trees (as well as shrubs), adding wood to strengthen weak spots or to balance a load.

The ability to make wood is unique to woody plants and allows trees to be the world's tallest living organisms. Considering that some trees can live for centuries, it seems a sound survival strategy. A tree's woody framework, which is made up of trunk, branches, and twigs, allows it to hold its leaves higher than other plants' leaves, giving them good light exposure and keeping them at a safe distance from disturbances on the ground, such as grazing animals, fire, and floodwaters.

## The Role of Leaves and Chlorophyll

Leaves and needles develop from buds on the branches. Their characteristic green color comes from chlorophyll, the pigment essential for photosynthesis, the process by which leaves capture the sun's energy and transform it into carbohydrates. Some photosynthesis can occur just beneath the outer bark, but most carbohydrates are made in the leaves.

Leaves also play an important role in transpiration, the movement of water through a tree. Trees take up water through the roots, move it up the trunk or stems through the tubelike water-conducting cells of the xylem, and out of the leaves through pores on the undersides called stomates (guard cells). By opening and closing the stomates, trees control water uptake and loss.

Trees also use the stomates to absorb carbon dioxide from the air. If conditions are right, water and carbon dioxide combine in the leaf through photosynthesis to form sugar. As part of the process the leaf also releases oxygen into the air. If air temperatures are too high, the tree closes the stomates to prevent large amounts of water from moving up and out through the leaves. However, with the stomates closed, no gas is exchanged and photosynthesis stops.

What's a tree to do? It can't move to a cooler place, but it can create its own shade. On the outer, exposed parts of its leaf canopy, a tree may make small, thin "sun leaves." On the inside of the canopy where the light is less intense, it grows "shade leaves," which may be larger and darker than sun leaves and contain more chlorophyll. When temperatures are high, the sun leaves close their stomates to conserve water, while the protected shade leaves continue to photosynthesize.

A healthy balance of sun and shade leaves is vital for the tree's well-being. If part of the outer canopy is removed, shade leaves may be exposed to brighter sunlight than they are prepared for, and they may get burned and stop photosynthesizing. Similarly, if large numbers of leaves are removed from the interior through branch loss or overzealous pruning, there won't be sufficient shade leaves to keep food production going on hot, sunny days. Therefore, understanding this growth pattern and the function of the leaves is vital for effective tree care.

Nature's solar collectors, leaves capture the sun's energy to make sugar, the basis of the earth's food supply.

## Root Matters

Being underground, roots are easily overlooked. They rightfully deserve as much attention as any other tree part, given that they make up 20 to 30 percent of a tree's mass, which is about the same percentage as the leaves. Most tree roots are found in the top 6 to 18 inches of soil, where water, nutrients, and oxygen are most accessible. Depending on the soil quality, a tree's root system can extend out two to three times beyond its canopy area. Roots anchor the tree, absorb and transport water and nutrients to the crown, and are the primary storage place for carbohydrates produced by the tree. Many health problems observed in the leaves and stems such as chlorotic, or yellow, leaves out of season and branch dieback from the tips are often related to root disorders.

Woody roots give a tree mechanical support, anchoring it into the earth. Like the trunk or stems, they have tubelike vessels that transport the liquids that are absorbed by the nonwoody roots. Woody roots are also the tree's piggy bank; this is where the tree stores its food reserves in the form of starches, oils, and fats. Like many other

plants, trees store their carbohydrates underground, where they are safer from poaching. Soil compaction, too much or too little water, disturbance from digging, and the addition of soil can all lead to root injury and promote diseases that may attack woody roots (as well as nonwoody ones) and compromise the roots' ability to anchor the tree.

Nonwoody roots are the workhorses of the root system: They absorb water and nutrients. Like leaves, these small roots don't last long; they are used for a season or two, then they are shed or become

**Roots absorb water and nutrients from the soil and anchor the tree to its site. They make up almost a third of the tree's mass, about the same as the leaves.**

part of the woody root system. Trees use root hairs and mycorrhizae for absorption. Root hairs are opportunistic and grow fast when conditions are right but will die off just as quickly when they aren't. Mycorrhiza describes a symbiotic relationship between root and fungi. There may be over 2,500 kinds of soil fungi that can form mycorrhizal relationships with trees. The fungi infect the nonwoody tree roots and increase their total area for absorption many times over. Mycorrhizae facilitate the uptake of water and minerals, particularly phosphorus, and in return, the fungi receive carbohydrate exudates from the tree. Mycorrhizal associations are important for tree health. Poor soil conditions, compaction, and fungicides can all have negative effects on the soil fungi.

## How Tree Age Informs Tree Care

Appropriate care for a tree depends largely on its age. Though this may sound straightforward, the tree's chronologic age—the amount of time that has elapsed since it was a seedling—may not tell you much about the tree's stage of development or decline. Some trees, like willows (*Salix* species), naturally put much of their resources into fast growth to stay ahead of their competition, while others, like oaks (*Quercus* species), grow more slowly but allocate more resources to fend off pests and diseases. To allow for differences in growth patterns among tree species and the impact of variable environmental conditions on tree health, botanists have devised two other ways to capture the essence of a tree's aging process, the ontogenetic age and the physiological age.

### THE ONTOGENETIC AGE OF A TREE

Botanists refer to a tree's ontogenetic age to specify its growth phase and to distinguish between different life stages. These are reflected in the chapters on care for trees in their formative, mature, and veteran years. Different species of trees remain in each phase for different lengths of time. Willows progress from seedling to maturity in just a few decades, while oaks may take up to a hundred years to reach maturity. This is important to keep in mind when assessing the kind of care a tree needs. A 20-year-old willow could be treated as a mature tree, while an oak of the same age should be treated as a juvenile. Regardless of the type of tree, growth and vitality inevitably decline over the tree's lifetime, and its maintenance requirements change, including pruning needs, one of the most serious concerns for caregivers.

The first step to good tree care is determining its ontogenetic age, or life phase, rather than its chronologic age. Each species progresses from the formative stage to maturity and senescence at a different pace, and individual trees age differently depending on their environment. Above are a juvenile yellowwood (left) and an early mature black locust.

## The Stages of Ontogenetic Age

**Formative Stage:** *Seedling to juvenile to early maturity*

- Fast root and stem growth enhanced by mycorrhizal root associations
- Low volume of deadwood or dysfunctional tissues
- High vitality—lots of energy and good overall health
- Close to 100 percent living tissue (or dynamic mass)


**Mature Stage:** *Full maturity to late maturity*

- Tree reaches its full potential size or optimal crown size
- Amount of food produced by leaves each year remains stable
- Growth slows and top growth becomes more outward or lateral than upward
- Tips grow more laterally than vertically
- Onset of natural limb loss
- Increase in dysfunctional tissues (or static mass)
- Decaying wood present, caused by fungal growth either on the outside of the tree or under sunken spots on the trunk or branches
- 50 percent or less dynamic mass

Once you have ascertained your tree's life stage, you can tailor its care to its needs. For the trees above, a mature sugar maple (left) and a veteran blue oak, little interference is necessary beyond keeping their soil from becoming compacted and pruning dangerous limbs or deadwood.

**Veteran Stage:** *Early ancient to late ancient to senescent*

- Crown dieback
- Branch loss
- Damage and decay to stems and roots
- Slow growth
- Low energy due to leaf-area decline
- Terminal decline leading to death

Note: For trees with strong defense systems such as oaks, this may the longest life stage.

## THE PHYSIOLOGICAL AGE OF A TREE

Botanists talk about a tree's physiological age to describe its general condition and its balance of vigor and decline, or growing tissues and dying parts. A young tree that has been badly damaged in a nursery can be as deeply in decline and low on energy as an ancient tree. To get a sense of a tree's vigor, look at its growing tips in late spring. The average shade tree will put on 6 to 12 inches of new growth at the tips each year.

The most important thing to remember is that each tree needs care appropriate for its species, age, growing conditions, and overall health. By understanding the survival strategies of different trees, their structural development, and their environmental requirements, you can do your part to promote a long and healthy life for all your trees.

# Tree Business

To better understand how a tree works, try thinking of a tree as a business. Each tree produces sugars—its "capital"—which fuel its growth and other physiological processes by transforming light energy from the sun, carbon dioxide from the air, and water from the soil into carbohydrates. This remarkable process, photosynthesis, occurs in the leaves. From there, carbohydrates are moved to the trunk and roots for storage. Trees invest their capital, or stored energy, in six major functions:

Respiration: Plant (and animal) cells burn energy—respire—to keep all their processes functioning. Respiration is comparable to a tree paying its utility bills. As trees get bigger, so do their respiration costs.

Growth: Trees grow throughout their lives, but they put more or less energy toward growth at different stages. Young trees grow faster than mature trees, which spend more energy building supportive material for their greater height and bulk.

Reproduction: Trees produce flowers and fruit to entice other organisms to move their pollen and seeds around. Anchored in place, trees are reliant on pollinators and seed vectors to disperse pollen and seed (except for the species whose pollen and/or seed are dispersed by the wind). Flowering and fruiting are biologically very expensive processes—but they are effective.

Defense: Trees protect themselves from pest and disease attacks by producing chemical compounds that repel them; they fight off infection by walling off affected areas from the healthy part of the tree through compartmentalization. These defenses are necessary for a tree's health, but they also require more energy because the compounds are much more complex than the basic sugars they usually produce.

Exudation: Trees feed the soil they are anchored in by diffusing carbohydrates, amino acids, organic acids, and inorganic ions through their roots. Between 5 percent and 40 percent of a tree's resources are exuded through the roots. These exudates nourish the soil organisms that promote the tree's health.

Storage: Trees store carbohydrates in their root system and trunk, or stem, and use this energy to produce leaves and insure against drought and other environmental stresses.

As trees progress through life, they allocate their resources in different ways. Young trees spend more energy on growth than on defense and reproduction. As trees mature, defense and reproduction take precedence over growth. Young trees need only a little capital to get started, and if they are efficient and have the right opportunities, they can make a big return on that investment, putting a lot of the energy they produce into storage for hard times. The larger a tree's savings, the better its chances of surviving a setback—or series of setbacks.

As trees grow larger, their expenses increase as well, and their profit margins—the energy they can put away—get smaller. Mature trees make just enough energy to support themselves, getting by until something comes along that eats away at their savings: drought, a pest or disease outbreak, or overzealous pruning, for example.

When a mature tree's energy savings have already been depleted through previous setbacks, a particularly bad year could be its last. A tree that experiences many setbacks over time will start cutting back, just as a business would, by downsizing or saving energy in other ways. Trees downsize by shedding leaves, branches, and even roots to reduce their energy use. Downsizing is a tree's last defense. By reducing its energy needs, a tree may live longer with less.

As generating systems, trees keep on growing up until they die. Each season they add new mass during a life cycle that for many species may span centuries. Their chances of a long life are greatest in a suitable environment such as a forest habitat, the place where most tree species have evolved and to which they are supremely adapted.

# The Perfect Match: The Right Tree in the Right Place

Planting a tree is a gift that connects us to future generations. It ensures that there will be a living canopy around our homes and neighborhoods in coming years as old trees die or are removed. Planting trees is also a big responsibility: If you place a tree in an unsuitable location, some time in the future someone may have to make a tough decision about its fate. A very large conifer like a Colorado blue spruce or a large deciduous tree like an oak sited too close to a building or underneath utility lines will most likely be cut back substantially or removed before it can reach its full grandeur. A tree installed in soil that doesn't meet its needs may never develop to its ultimate potential, going into slow decline instead. A street tree carelessly stuck in the ground and neglected after planting may struggle for years and turn into a hazardous eyesore instead of a natural beauty providing much needed shade.

Matching a tree to its site is the single most important factor for growing it successfully. A tree can't get up and move to better ground. Planted in a spot poorly suited to its needs, it will put a lot of energy toward adapting. If it does not succeed it will inevitably decline and die. To avoid this scenario, familiarize yourself with the features of your site and spend some time carefully selecting a tree appropriate for it. You will reap the rewards later, as you watch a gangly youngster grow to graceful maturity with minimal intervention from you or anyone else.

**A tree that's well matched to its home will develop into a healthy mature specimen, like this *Chamaecyparis obtusa* 'Nana Gracilis', whose growing preferences and potential height and spread—of both its branches and roots—were considered before it was planted near a building.**

## Assessing the Features of the Planting Site

The first step toward growing a tree successfully is site assessment: a close survey of all above- and below-ground conditions relevant for tree growth. Once you have examined the features of your site, you can look for good candidate trees for it. Going through this process step by step, as outlined below, doesn't take long. For easy reference on location, use the site-assessment checklist on page 31 to guide you. (A printer-friendly version of the checklist is on the BBG website at www.bbg.org/treecareprimer.) Then turn to page 102 for a list of trees for specific situations.

### EXISTING STRUCTURES

Take a walk around the area where you want to plant a tree and take note of the location of structures already in place, such as buildings and foundations, walls,

fences, overhead wires, and buried utility lines, as well as other trees and shrubs. Bear in mind that a tree can live a long time; try to visualize how it will grow into the available space over the years. Take in the whole picture and consider how the site could change: Might it be altered in the future by a new building project or the addition of a walkway or new plantings? Also consider whether the tree will eventually shade other plants. Making a rough sketch of the property's permanent features and then blocking out the spaces available for a mature tree gives you a better idea of how a tree will fit into the space and how it will alter it over time.

Removing a tree that ended up in the wrong spot can be far more costly in time and money than using a little foresight before planting.

### SPACE MATTERS ABOVE AND BELOW GROUND

One of the biggest—and most overlooked—needs of landscape and city trees is adequate space to accommodate their growth. It is very easy to underestimate the substantial amounts of space above and below ground that a tree occupies as it expands over the years. When it comes to giving room to trees, the focus tends to be on their

**Providing shade and privacy as well as vertical interest among the other plants, this small crabapple, *Malus × zumi,* is in scale with the building and a good match for this intimate setting.**

above-ground size and branching patterns. But it's just as important to consider the root system underground. Out of view, and usually out of mind, roots make up almost a third of a tree's mass. Trees need a serious amount of underground real estate. Unfettered by subterranean obstacles, their root zones easily spread far beyond the tree's drip line, the perimeter of the tree's branches. If roots are curtailed by obstacles that inhibit their spread, the amount of water, nutrients, and oxygen to which they have access will be limited. As you do your site assessment, carefully check for underground structures, buried utilities, compacted soils near curbs and driveways, and other factors that could restrict a tree's root growth. Research done by Gary Watson of the Morton Arboretum in Lisle, Illinois, has shown that a 50-foot-tall tree can have a root zone that is over 100 feet in diameter. In the study, roots were found mainly in the top three feet of soil, with most nonwoody roots less than one foot beneath the surface. Think of a household candle stuck to a dinner plate, and you get an idea of the root plate model. There may be some exceptions to this model, depending on soil type and tree species, but it's a useful picture to keep in mind when figuring out how much root space a tree may need over its life span.

## LIGHT PATTERNS

All trees use the sun's light as an energy source, but different trees require different amounts of direct sunlight. Some prefer full sun and others perform best in full shade, but many trees tolerate a broad range of light conditions. Most dogwoods (*Cornus* species), for example, are understory trees that naturally grow in spots that offer a fair amount of shade. As landscape specimens, however, they are often planted in full sun because that's where they produce the most flowers. (Interestingly, a dogwood's attractive bloom doesn't indicate good health: It is a sign that the tree is stressed. More flowers mean more seeds, which in turn assure better chances of survival for the species—but often at the expense of the individual tree's health.)

Take the time to observe how much light the area gets where you would like to plant. Unless the spot is completely in the open, the amount of available sunlight probably varies substantially from morning to evening and over the course of the year. Your house or other buildings, as well as nearby hills and other natural features, may also shade different parts of the site as the seasons change.

Once you've determined how many hours of sunlight the site gets each day, choose a tree naturally adapted to that amount of available light. Conversely, if you have a particular tree you want to plant, find out its sunlight requirements and try to find a site that matches its needs. Plant labels in the nursery usually indicate sunlight requirements: "Full sun" means the tree requires at least six hours of direct sunlight each day; "partial sun/partial shade" means it needs three to six hours of sun each day, preferably in the morning and early afternoon; and "full shade" means it requires fewer than three hours of direct sunlight each day.

## Understand the Soil: Structure, Nutrients, pH, Drainage

**Structure** Soil structure is an important factor for tree health because it determines how easily a tree can spread its roots. Most trees do best in loose crumbly soils like those found in forests, the native habitat of most trees. Such conditions can be a far cry from the bare, rock-solid soils often encountered in cities or suburban areas.

To get an idea of the composition of the soil at your site, take a spade or shovel and dig down a foot. Rub the soil between your fingers. What does it feel like? Soil is composed of sand, silt, clay, and organic matter. The small particles of sand and silt are bound by clay and organic matter into aggregates. These are the crumbs or lumps the soil breaks into when you dig it. The arrangement of aggregates gives soil its structure. In the spaces between soil particles there are small pockets of air, with more air

**Insert a steel probe, or even a pencil, into the soil as a quick and simple way to check for compaction. If the soil is not compacted, the probe should easily go in six inches or more.**

found in the top layer of soil, where most root growth occurs. When the soil structure is good, there are adequate spaces between aggregates to allow free flow of air and water into the soil. This type of soil is easy to dig into. It feels loose and crumbly to the touch and drains easily. But it is also able to hold some moisture—essential for maintaining plant growth. Tree roots can easily penetrate the soil and are able to absorb oxygen needed for respiration, the process by which the plant's cells release energy from their carbohydrate stores to fuel their growth and other processes. When the soil structure is poor, as in soil compacted by heavy foot traffic, you will have a hard time getting your spade into it because there are few aggregates and the air pockets, or pore spaces, between them are very, very small. In these conditions roots may be unable to access the oxygen they need and trees can literally suffocate. However, all is not lost if you encounter such conditions in your yard. Some trees do quite well in less than perfect soils. Hackberries (*Celtis* species) and hawthorns (*Crataegus* species), for example, have tough, vigorous root systems highly adaptable to many different soil conditions, which make them useful candidates for compacted sites.

**Nutrients** In addition to the elements necessary for photosynthesis, trees need 13 mineral nutrients found in the soil. The three it requires in most abundance are nitrogen, phosphorus, and potassium. The only precise way to determine how much of

A tree species needs to be adapted to the available water. Bald cypress, *Taxodium distichum*, is one of the few trees that survives in standing water.

each is available at your site is to perform a soil nutrient analysis. Most states' cooperative extension services have soil labs, which will analyze a soil sample for a small fee and give you a detailed breakdown of your soil's composition.

If you have some plant knowledge or gardening experience, you can get a basic idea of your soil's fertility and condition by observing what kinds of plants are growing well nearby. For example, the presence of plants considered weeds in your area often indicates that the soil has been disturbed, which some types of trees cannot tolerate. In this case, pick a species that flourishes in a wide range of soil conditions. Moisture-loving plants indicate that the site is wet, making it suitable for trees that thrive with lots of water and that may tolerate waterlogged soil. If you see plants that display signs of possible trouble, like yellowing leaves and stunted or abnormal growth patterns, and suspect that these may be due to a soil problem, or if you are unfamiliar with the plants growing on the site, your best bet is to start with a professional soil analysis.

Soil pH—Alkaline, Neutral, or Acidic Soil When you send a soil sample to a lab for analysis, you will learn its pH level, but you can also determine it with a simple test kit available at garden centers. The soil pH tells you whether your soil is alkaline (pH above 7), neutral (pH 7), or acidic (pH below 7). This is important to know; although some trees can tolerate a wide pH range, some species have very specific requirements. Pin oaks (*Quercus palustris*), for example, have difficulty absorbing iron in alkaline soil. Even if iron is present, they will develop the yellowed leaves of chlorosis in these conditions. Many conifers are adapted to acidic soil and may suffer nutrient deficiencies if the soil is not quite right for them. If you'd like to plant a tree in a lawn, there are a number of soil issues to be aware of. See "Trees and Lawns," page 30.

Drainage How much water is available to the tree roots depends on the structure of the soil and how well it drains. You can determine whether soil drains freely or holds water by doing a simple field percolation test. Dig a hole about one foot deep and wide and fill it with water. Let the water drain completely. Refill the hole and measure the depth of the water after 15 minutes. Calculate the rate of drainage in inches per hour. When drainage is poor, the water level goes down four inches per hour; when it is moderate, four to eight inches per hour; and when

A percolation test indicates soil structure and therefore compaction. Dig a hole one foot deep and wide, fill it with water, and let it drain. Then fill it again and measure how long it takes to drain.

it is excessive, eight or more inches per hour. Poor drainage is quite common in suburban yards and urban areas as soils become compressed during construction or by continuous heavy foot traffic. In these situations it is usually much better to pick a tree that does well in this type of soil than try to correct a drainage problem.

## Healthy Soil and Compaction

Soil that is alive and healthy gives trees a much better chance of long-term success. Healthy soil is an ecosystem unto itself, composed of both mineral and living particles. Sand, silt, and clay make up the mineral fraction of the soil. Organic matter made up of decomposing plant and animal residues holds the mineral particles together and helps maintain the soil food web—the organisms that decompose matter, bind nutrients for plants, and aerate the soil.

Over time, as soil particles weather down, nutrients are released into the soil, mainly from clay and organic matter. Dissolved in water, the nutrients are absorbed by tree roots in the biologically active zone around the roots known as the rhizosphere.

To understand what happens when soil becomes compacted, it helps to have a sense of how the various constituents of soil work together. To visualize the mineral compo-

A core aerator relieves compaction as it pulls out small plugs of soil and allows air in. It is most effective when turf is removed and the area is mulched after aeration.

nent of soil, imagine a large clear bowl filled with a mix of basketballs (playing the role of sand), softballs (silt), and golf balls (clay). Inside the bowl you'll see lots of spaces between the balls. If there are many basketballs in the bowl, the spaces are large, which minimizes cohesion, and water poured over them drains fast (equivalent to sandy soils). If there are mostly golf balls, there is less space between particles, and water moves more slowly (clay soils). In soil, the pore spaces between mineral particles are all-important for tree health because they provide room for air, water, and roots to move though the soil. Pore space also provides room for the living organisms of the soil food web.

Imagine placing a heavy weight on top of the balls in the bowl. As they start to flatten out, the air spaces become fewer and farther between, which is exactly what happens to soil when it becomes compacted. In compacted soil, water and air cannot move, and living organisms die. Tree roots cannot absorb water and nutrients and cannot grow.

Soil compaction is difficult to remedy without drastic measures and should be prevented whenever possible. To limit soil compaction, discourage or restrict foot traffic around trees—by mulching, establishing shade-tolerant plants under the tree, or even fencing off the tree. If the soil has already been compacted, first try core aeration, then spread a thin layer of organic matter like compost and organic mulch over the surface. It will work its way into the soil and alleviate compaction over time. For very badly compacted soils, radial trenching and vertical mulching may provide relief. Both methods are minimally invasive techniques used to remove old soil and replace it with compost or other materials. Both can improve aeration and sometimes fertility in compacted soils. Radial trenching is done by an arborist with an air spade, a handheld lance-like

**Many types of trees tend to grow best when planted in groups, with understory trees partially shaded by canopy species, as they would be in a natural forest habitat.**

tool connected to a portable high-pressure compressor. The arborist uses the air spade—which produces a powerful jet of air that blasts the soil—to dig a series of trenches about a foot deep, radiating from the base of the trunk flare like the spokes of a wheel as far out as is practical, but at least ten feet. The tool doesn't damage woody roots, and although fine root hairs are often blasted away, they quickly recolonize. The pulverized soil is removed, amended with organic matter, and replaced in the trench. Contaminated soil should be removed outright and replaced with fresh soil. For vertical mulching, start by drilling holes 12 to 18 inches deep around the tree's root zone, using a 2- to 4-inch soil auger or posthole digger. Dig holes about three to four feet apart, then amend and replace soil. This technique is not recommended for trees with very shallow root systems, such as maples (*Acer*), American larch (*Larix laricina*), and river birch (*Betula nigra*).

## Water Issues

Trees, like humans, need to stay hydrated to maintain all cellular functions. Photosynthesis and respiration, and therefore growth, can't take place without water. Water is just as essential for the soil microorganisms on which trees depend. You can find out how much rain falls in your area on the website of the National Weather Service or by calling your local cooperative extension office. Plant only trees adapted to live with the water that's available naturally during the course of the year. You should, of course, water and mulch newly planted trees as needed to avoid drought stress, but don't plan on watering trees over the long term. If you have a mature tree that isn't getting enough water naturally, it was planted in the wrong site. If you live in an area normally prone to drought, plant species that are tolerant of dry conditions.

You can have too much of a good thing, however: Waterlogged soils can be deadly to many trees. But there are also many species that grow well in wet soil. An excellent example is the bald cypress (*Taxodium distichum*), a native of southern swamps that can grow with its roots underwater.

## Prevailing Winds

Take a site's prevailing wind patterns into account when deciding what type of tree to plant and where. Some trees are structurally better suited to a windy spot than others. Stronger-wooded trees such as oaks (*Quercus* species), lindens (*Tilia* species), and plane trees (*Platanus* species) stand up better to fierce winds than trees with weaker wood like willows (*Salix* species), white pine (*Pinus alba*), and plums (*Prunus* species). Evergreen trees like firs (*Abies* species), spruces (*Picea* species), and even southern magnolia (*Magnolia grandiflora*) can act as valuable windscreens.

Strong wind can be very damaging; it can desiccate trees, pulling water from their leaves more quickly than the trees can replace it through their roots. Near the ocean, strong winds may also carry salt spray, which can be damaging to many trees. Some trees have evolved in this type of climate, such as honeylocust (*Gleditsia triacanthos*) and sweetbay (*Magnolia virginiana*), and are able to tolerate these conditions.

## Temperatures

**Hardiness Zones** In addition to all their other requirements, trees have temperature ranges that they can tolerate comfortably. The minimum winter temperatures that common landscape trees and other plants are able to withstand are designated as their hardiness zone range, expressed by the U.S. Department of Agriculture as a number between 1 (northern Canada) and 11 (southern Mexico). This information is readily available in gardening reference materials and usually noted on nursery tags. Check the map on page 112 to learn your area's USDA hardiness zone, and keep it in mind when choosing trees. While you should always plant trees suited to your climate, you should not base your decision solely on hardiness.

**Microclimates** Learn to take advantage of microclimates, small zones where the temperature is above or below the normal surrounding temperatures. A south-facing wall, for example, absorbs heat as the sun hits it throughout the day, then gradually releases that heat, creating a warmer microclimate than that found a few feet away. Here you might succeed in growing a tree that is not cold hardy in your area. In the same way, you can grow a tree with a low tolerance for wind in an otherwise blustery location by sheltering it with other trees and shrubs. A warmer or cooler microclimate can be a great place to experiment with trees that might not otherwise thrive in your zone.

## Finding a Suitable Tree

Once you have familiarized yourself with the features of your site, check with local nurseries and garden centers to identify trees that match your size range, your hardiness zone, your soil—and of course, your aesthetic preferences. Try to visit a few local botanical gardens or arboreta to see a variety of regionally adapted trees at different life stages. These preparations will help you make an informed choice about what trees to plant and where. Also, see "Choosing Trees," page 98, for suggestions.

Consider future planting or building projects as well as proximity to existing structures when siting a tree. Once established, most trees resent disturbance.

# Trees and Lawns

The large specimen tree in the middle of a perfect, rolling lawn is an enduring legacy of British landscape design. But what lawns need from the soil to make them thick and healthy is usually the opposite of what a tree needs.

Many grasses are native to prairie ecosystems, whose soils tend to have a higher pH than forest soils. The soil pH level recommended for most lawns is 7 or higher (neutral or alkaline) but in a forest ecosystem, the habitat of most tree species, the soil is typically acidic. The classic tree-in-lawn scenario is a pH nightmare unless you choose a tree species that is compatible with the needs of the grass. Trees such as bur oak (*Quercus macrocarpa*), American linden (*Tilia americana*), and hackberries (*Celtis* species) are adapted to soils with a higher pH level. They are native to the prairie soils of the Midwest, which tend to be somewhat alkaline, due to ancient limestone deposits in the region.

Even if you choose well, a tree planted in a lawn is still up against root competition, lawn mower damage, and possibly fungicide and pesticide applications for the grass—though these are best avoided for the sake of all living things, not just trees.

The biggest problem is that homeowners often pay much more attention to the health of their grass than that of their trees. Grass shows short-term stress faster and more dramatically than a tree, so there is a tendency to pamper the grass and forget about the long-term effects that our actions may have on trees.

To create better growing conditions for the grass, people often thin out their trees. But it's not just the *amount* of shade that makes it hard to grow turf under trees. The main problem is the *quality* of the light that plants receive there. As sunlight passes

through a tree's canopy, much of the red and blue light gets filtered and absorbed by the leaves. Removing some of the lower branches to allow more light to pass under the canopy produces a much better result than thinning. An even better strategy is to mulch widely around the tree's trunk, keeping grass well away from the tree. This is good for the tree, and the lawn will be healthier and greener growing in areas suited to it.

**Surround a tree planted in a lawn with mulch to help keep moisture in, feed the soil, and keep the lawn mower away from the trunk.**

# Site Assessment and Planning Checklist for New Tree Plantings

Location_____ Date_____

Side of house (north, south, northeast, etc.)_____ Hardiness zone_____

Microclimate windy_____frost pocket_____reflected heat_____other_____

Irrigation system ☐ Y ☐ N Supplemental irrigation ☐ Y ☐ N Average rainfall_____

Light levels full sun_____partial shade_____full shade_____

Are there existing trees or plantings? ☐ Y ☐ N

Species_____Size_____Condition (good, fair, poor)_____

**Above-Ground Space Available**

Distance from other plantings & trees_____

Distance from buildings/structures_____

Distance from neighboring properties_____

Overhead wires ☐ Y ☐ N (If so, how high?)_____

**Below-Ground Space Available**

Rooting space length_____width_____depth_____(It is important to dig to examine soil.)

Are there stumps or roots from other trees or plantings? ☐ Y ☐ N

Are there any below-ground utility cables or pipes? ☐ Y ☐ N

**Soil and Drainage**

pH levels_____Soil texture: clayey_____loamy_____sandy_____

Compaction levels before planting: no compaction_____moderate_____severe_____

Heavily used area with possible soil compaction after planting? ☐ Y ☐ N

Drainage wet_____well drained_____dry_____

Possible use of de-icing salts on site_____possible soil erosion_____flooding_____

Noxious weeds_____

**Other Soil or Site Problems**_____

**Installation Considerations**

Access to planting site: clear path_____gates or fences_____(If so, how big?)_____

Other_____

Vehicle access_____

Will you need to lay plywood to protect turf or soil beds?_____

How much plywood will be needed?_____

If only access is through a building, check door sizes and openings_____

Will you need to add or remove soil from planting site? (If so, how much?)_____

Checklist courtesy of the Urban Horticulture Institute, Department of Horticulture, Cornell University. For a printer-friendly version of this checklist, visit the BBG website at www.bbg.org/treecareprimer.

# Buying a Tree

For most gardeners, myself included, a visit to a nursery or garden center is like a trip to the candy store: There are so many wonderfully enticing possibilities. To make the most of your visit, prepare yourself with all the information you can about your planting site (see "The Perfect Match," page 18, especially the site assessment checklist, page 31) and a short list of trees you want to grow. Many nurseries specialize in particular kinds of plants, so if you know exactly what you want, call ahead to be sure the nursery carries the tree you're looking for. If you plan to plant a very small tree, you may also be able to buy it from a reputable nursery online or through a mail-order catalog. Whenever possible, try to buy trees from nurseries that grow their stock in your geographic region. It is the best way to ensure that the plants are well adapted to the local climate.

## The Language of Tree Shopping

**Tree Sizes** Tree sizes are measured by height or by caliper, which is the diameter of the trunk measured near the ground (with tree calipers). Height is the common measure for deciduous trees up to eight feet tall and for all evergreen trees. Caliper measurement is used for deciduous trees more than ten feet tall. In the nursery trade, tree size increases by quarter-inch or half-inch caliper increments. For example, a tree with a 2.5-inch caliper has a trunk that measures 2½ inches in diameter at six inches above the ground. (Trees more than four inches in diameter are measured a foot above the ground.) Trees grown in containers are sold by pot size or by height.

**Balled and Burlapped (B&B)** This describes trees harvested by the method used for most field-grown trees. At harvest time, a sharp spade is used to cut through the roots

Not all nursery trees are created equal. Take your time to scrutinize the youngsters carefully, and choose a well-grown specimen with a strong leader and overall good branching pattern.

and dig a narrow trench in a circle around the base of the tree. This leaves a circular mass of soil and roots, which is then lifted out of the hole. Many nurseries use mechanical tree spades for the job. This may be more economical, but it is not as good for the tree as digging by hand. The root ball is covered with burlap and tied up or set in a wire basket so that it can be moved. Even though up to 90 percent of the root system may be lost in the process, small to very large trees are successfully transplanted this way. Large shade trees and other large specimens are often sold B&B, as the pros call it. They have extremely heavy root balls easily weighing several hundred pounds and need to be moved and planted using machinery such as a backhoe. Due to their large size, they cost more than smaller trees, and they also take longer to become established because of the substantial root loss at harvest.

**Container Grown** These are trees that have been grown in a pot rather than a field. Small flowering trees such as cherries and plums (*Prunus* species), dogwoods (*Cornus* species), and crabapples (*Malus* species) are often grown this way. Many nurseries have begun to grow even large trees such as oaks, maples, and other shade trees in pots because they take up less nursery space than they would growing in a field. Container-grown trees suffer only minor, if any, root loss when they are transplanted

and so will take more readily to their new site. Plants grown in the lightweight soil media used in pots are also generally easier to handle. On the downside, if the nursery is not vigilant about upgrading trees to larger pots as the trees develop, their roots may end up circling the rootball, making the tree pot-bound. Circling roots of pot-bound trees need to be teased out when the tree is planted, or they may strangle it. Because of their more extensive root

**Keep weight in mind when picking a B&B tree. One cubic foot of soil may easily weigh 100 pounds.**

system, all container plants need more frequent watering after planting, especially during their first season.

**Bare Root** This old planting method is becoming popular again, mainly for smaller deciduous trees and for trees sold by mail order. In this approach, the nursery digs up a field-grown tree and combs the soil out of the roots. The buyer gets a tree with a good-sized root system but doesn't have to wrestle with—or pay postage for—a hefty root ball. Bare-root trees are especially vulnerable to desiccation and should be planted quickly. The roots need to be kept moist at all times until they are back in the ground.

**When dug out to be balled and burlapped, a tree loses a substantial amount of roots, as this "nude" example shows. It usually takes more time to get established than a container-grown or bare-root tree.**

**Easily Transplanted** This term is used to describe trees that adapt well after being dug up and moved and that quickly establish a new root system. Ash trees (*Fraxinus* species) belong in this category. They have a very fibrous root system that grows back quickly.

**Fall Transplant** This term describes trees that do well when dug and replanted in fall. According to arborists at Cornell University, trees like sugar maple (*Acer saccharum*) and lindens (*Tilia* species) do better when planted in fall; their rate of root growth is higher, and their stem diameter increases more quickly than in trees planted in spring.

For nurseries, fall planting has the advantage of extending the selling season. Home gardeners may have more time to plant and care for their new trees in fall than during the spring gardening rush. It should be noted, however, that most evergreen trees are not suited for fall planting. They do best when they are dug up and replanted in spring.

# Types of Trees

Nurseries often group trees into categories that can be helpful in understanding tree types and how they might best be used in the landscape.

**Shade Trees** are typically large trees (50 feet or taller at maturity) with a high canopy that will give a fair amount of shade and have open space underneath. Elms (*Ulmus* species), white oak (*Quercus alba*), and sugar maple (*Acer saccharum*) are all shade trees. They should be planted where there is plenty of space above and below ground for them to develop their proper forms and canopy sizes.

**Ornamental Trees** can be of any size and have at least one outstanding, attractive feature—superior fall color, like maples (*Acer* species); interesting bark leaves, or flowers, like Korean dogwood (*Cornus kousa*); unusual form, like weeping cherries (*Prunus* cultivars); or showy fruit, like hawthorns (*Crataegus* species).

**Flowering Trees** are, simply put, trees with showy flowers—magnolias, crabapples (*Malus* species and cultivars), and cherries (*Prunus* species and cultivars) are a few popular varieties. Note that many other trees not commonly labeled as flowering trees in the trade nevertheless have appealing, elegant flowers, though possibly more delicate and best appreciated at close range. Some examples are tulip tree (*Liriodendron tulipifera*), red maple (*Acer rubrum*), and lindens (*Tilia* species). Consider bloom color and timing with respect to the color of your house and other plantings in the vicinity.

**Specimen Trees** are outstanding or rare trees with attractive features and/or form, such as Japanese maple (*Acer palmatum*). They may be specially trained or pruned, such as a *Stewartia* pruned to highlight its ornamental bark, and are often sited to showcase their features, such as a carefully groomed pine in a Japanese garden. They tend to be more expensive than other trees.

**Korean dogwood, *Cornus kousa*, is a small understory tree with showy flowers.**

## Size Matters

You may be tempted to splurge a little and buy a larger-sized tree to fill out an empty spot faster. Remember that in order to make bigger trees manageable, nurseries often remove up to 90 percent of the root systems of trees with a diameter of two inches or more. Their larger size makes them unwieldy, and they may require heavy equipment for moving and planting, all of which adds to their cost. Smaller trees are often the smarter choice. They are harvested with more of their root system intact, which should help them get established and adapted to the planting site more quickly. And they are, of course, easier to manage at planting time. Smaller nursery trees often outgrow larger ones that are planted at the same time.

**Stay away from nursery trees with headed-back branches like this poorly pruned specimen.**

## Tips for Selecting a Nursery Tree

- Choose a healthy tree with a well-developed trunk and well-placed lateral branches, and avoid ones that look as if they have been poorly pruned or topped.
- Look for healthy, moist buds, leaves, and stems and avoid trees with any sign of wounds in the bark.
- Choose a tree that has been freshly harvested. Recently dug trees tend to be more robust than those dug from a field months ago and are less likely to have a dying root ball. Most trees are dug in early spring or in fall—if you're buying a tree in August, chances are good that it is not freshly dug. Old, weathered burlap around a root ball is another clue that a tree has been out of the ground for a while.

- Make sure that the tree's trunk flair is visible above the soil line. The trunk flare is the area where the roots branch from the trunk. If you can't see it, the tree was planted too deeply and may not have a healthy, well-developed root system.
- Ask if the tree has been root-pruned. Trees that are root-pruned by the nursery tend to have a better, more fibrous root system and will become established more quickly once planted.
- Ask the nursery if you may ease the tree from its container or cut open the burlap to expose some of the roots. Make sure that the roots are white and moist, indicating that they're free of disease and have been kept hydrated.
- When buying a container-grown tree, check for circling roots, which indicate that the tree hasn't been moved to a larger pot as needed and will not easily establish a healthy root system once planted.

## Getting the Tree Home

Once you've chosen your tree, there's the matter of getting it home. Many garden centers will deliver trees that are too large and heavy for a homeowner to transport in a car. If the tree fits in your car and you are planning to take it home yourself, don't leave it in the vehicle too long. Make your other stops before going to the nursery so that you don't delay getting home with the tree. If part of it protrudes from the trunk,

---

### Problem Nursery Trees

Beware of nursery trees that look like miniature versions of mature trees. Their lush growth and full crown may well be the result of careless pruning. Instead of carefully thinning out branches, nurseries sometimes prune trees by cutting the tips off the main stem and all the limbs, treating them essentially as if they were oversize basil plants. Unfortunately, the trees respond pretty much in the same way as basil: They sprout out profusely. Nurseries do this because it makes the young trees look more like mature trees. It also allows them to accommodate more trees in the same space because they can grow them more closely together; and for large nurseries that prune thousands of trees, heading back limbs is quicker than painstakingly thinning out individual branches by hand. It may be easy for the nurseries, but it's not good for young trees. A tree that has been headed back can develop competing leaders—two stems both trying to be the main trunk—and poor branch attachments. This changes the tree's natural shape and weakens it, making it prone to storm damage later in life. If you have a tree that has been treated in this way, you should start corrective pruning to guide its structural development. (See "Trees in Their Formative Years," page 56.)

## Tree Sizes and Weights

| Deciduous Trees | | Evergreen Trees | |
| --- | --- | --- | --- |
| Size | Weight of Root Ball | Size | Weight of Root Ball |
| 5 to 6 feet | 55 pounds | 3 feet | 90 pounds |
| 6 to 8 feet | 90 pounds | 4 feet | 130 pounds |
| 8 to 10 feet | 130 pounds | 5 feet | 225 pounds |
| 1.25-inch caliper | 185 pounds | | |
| 1.5-inch caliper | 225 pounds | | |
| 2-inch caliper | 390 pounds | | |

cover the top of the tree to avoid windburn—the desiccation of leaves—using a burlap cover or other material that will allow air to circulate around the tree. Avoid using plastic if possible.

Moving a tree can be backbreaking work. If it's too heavy, get help! Always pick up a tree by its pot or root ball. Never lift your tree by its trunk, because the weight of the root ball or container could tear the roots away from the trunk. Landscapers use spe-cial handcarts or straps that lift from the bottom to move large balled and burlapped trees. Because moving trees can be tricky, smaller or bare-root trees are sometimes a bet-ter choice than larger balled and burlapped specimens.

If you are not planting it right away, put your tree in a shady spot and keep it watered so its roots don't dry out. Bare-root trees are especially vulner-able because their entire root system is exposed to the air, so keep their roots moist and plant them as soon as possible.

**Fairly easy to manage at planting time, small nursery trees keep most of their root systems intact and catch up fast with larger balled and burlapped trees.**

# Planting a Tree

Planting a tree is hard work, but it can provide years of reward as generations to come enjoy the fruits of your labor. Two of the most important goals when planting are to get the tree in at the right depth and to keep it from drying out while it becomes established in its new home. When you are ready to plant:

- Dig a planting hole that is three to five times the diameter of the root ball or container and just deep enough to accommodate the roots. Find your tree's trunk flare, which is the area where the first roots branch from the trunk. If you are planting a balled and burlapped tree, remove enough of the burlap to expose it. Measure the height from the base of the trunk flare to the bottom of the root ball. That gives you the right planting depth.

- Remove a container-grown tree from its pot, then separate and spread out its roots. Then measure the height of the root ball.

- Prune back as many root tips as you can to promote a healthy, fibrous root system. Always make a clean cut to a moist, healthy part of the root.

- When setting the tree in the hole, make sure its trunk flare lies above ground level. It's much safer to plant a little too high than to plant too low and bury the trunk flare. As the soil settles in the weeks following planting, the tree will ease a little deeper into the ground.

- If you are planting a balled and burlapped tree, remove all lacing and wire and as much of the burlap as you can at this time. If left in place, these materials will impede the natural growth of the tree; wire can even girdle its root system over time.

**Planted along a public roadway, this young tree promises shade, beauty, and wildlife habitat among other benefits. A large bed like this one gives the growing tree's roots much more room to spread out than most individual tree pits afford.**

Planting a container-grown tree: Dig a hole and check that it is the right depth for your tree. Remove the tree from its pot. Cut off any circling roots, which might otherwise girdle the tree later on. Then install the tree at the same depth that it grew in its pot and refill the hole.

- Check to be sure the tree is standing straight and then fill the hole with the same soil that came out of it when you started. Don't use improved soil to fill the hole— the tree needs to adapt to the soil naturally found in its root zone. Pack the soil lightly into the hole; don't tamp it down excessively.

- Water the new tree well but slowly. Thoroughly drench the soil around the tree to a few feet from the root ball.

- Stake the tree only if it can't stand up by itself. If staking is necessary, place the stake on the upwind side of the tree and use flexible ties. Install these fairly low, about a third to halfway up the trunk between the ground and the lowest branches. Newly planted trees will develop roots and trunk taper faster when they are not staked or at least staked in a way that allows the top of the tree to move in the wind, presumably because they are forced to stabilize themselves. Be sure to remove any ties after one growing season to prevent them from girdling the tree.

- Prune only dead or damaged limbs. Wait at least a year before making any other pruning cuts. Do not prune any branches to compensate for root loss. It may reduce photosynthesis and can greatly reduce root growth.

- Do not wrap the trunk. Once thought to be useful against sun scald and drying out, wrappings can actually provide a moist place for insects to shelter and can prevent the small amount of photosynthesis that normally takes place in the trunk.

- Do not amend the soil around a new tree or fertilize it unless the soil is lacking in some nutrients. Fertilizers can push the tree into unwanted top growth at a time when it needs to put all its energy toward root growth.
- Spread a good organic mulch two to three inches deep around the root zone, but keep it away from the trunk itself because it can invite rodents and hold moisture up against the bark and lead to rot. Mulch helps conserve soil moisture and keeps down competition from weeds. In addition, I like to give trees a little private space whenever possible, so I fence or rope off an area around the tree to keep people and larger animals away until the tree has been in the ground a few seasons and appears to be adapting well to its new home.

One last tip: Most trees have a symbiotic relationship with certain types of soil fungi that help them absorb water and other essential elements from the soil. The fungus infects the roots, forming an association with the root tips called mycorrhiza ("fungus-root"). This relationship is very important for the long-term health of the tree, so it's a good idea to care for the fungus in the soil as well as the tree. How do you encourage mycorrhizae in your new tree? By watering properly and applying mulch, you create an environment that's beneficial for the fungi. You can also help infect the soil with fungi by applying commercial inoculants, but you need to select the right type of inoculant for your tree species; different trees are infected by different fungi. You can also inoculate a tree by giving it a bit of soil collected from the base of an established tree of the same species. For example, if you

**Keeping the young tree well watered is your single most important maintenance task during its first year.**

are planting a sugar maple, find another one that's growing well nearby and carefully dig a few scoops of soil from the area immediately around it. Try to include some small, nonwoody roots with the soil, then spread the mix around the roots of your new tree in its planting hole.

Observe the newly planted tree for signs of stress. The number one problem is drought stress. Proper watering throughout the first year and perhaps beyond is critical. (For care as the tree grows, see "Trees in Their Formative Years," page 56.)

Sometimes, even if you've done everything right, a tree doesn't make it. There are lots of reasons for a young tree's decline and death, but the most common one is that its roots dried out at some point, perhaps when the tree was still at the nursery. I find it takes about two growing seasons to really know if a tree is going to take to the site. If it's still looking healthy after its third season, chances are good that it will survive.

**Planting a large balled and burlapped tree can take several people. Gauge the planting depth (to the trunk flare). Ease the tree into the hole, lifting it by its root ball, never the trunk. Then remove the burlap and wire. Head back as many tree roots as you can, then fill in the hole.**

## Transplanting a Juvenile Tree

If you realize that you have planted your tree in the wrong spot after all, you have time to move it while it is still in the early juvenile stage. But the sooner you move it the better. To move a tree successfully, you will have to dig it up with a root ball that's in proportion to the size of the tree. There should be a foot of root ball for every inch of trunk diameter. For example, if your tree has a trunk diameter of two inches (measured at six inches above ground), you should dig a root ball measuring two feet across. Landscaping firms use mechanical tree spades with

**Be sure that the trunk flare is visible when you plant: A tree whose trunk flare has been buried is likely to develop girdling roots that could deform its growth and even increase its chances of toppling in high winds.**

hydraulically powered blades that can dig up a root ball easily, but even then it's best to move a tree when it is small, because the size and weight of the root ball that the tree needs to reestablish itself increases substantially as the tree grows.

The time to transplant a deciduous tree is before it leafs out in spring or after it drops its leaves in fall, depending on the species. The time to transplant a conifer is in early spring before bud break. It is best to root prune all trees one or two years before transplanting to promote the development of fibrous roots within the root mass that will be moved. Use a sharp digging spade to cut through the roots in a circle that is a little smaller than the size of the rootball you will need to dig up. You only need to go as deep as the blade of the spade. Keep the tree well watered after root pruning.

# Growing Trees in Containers

If you don't have much space or good soil or have a hard time limiting yourself to species that can naturally grow in your garden, try growing trees in pots. Containers are a great way to add more green space around your home, inside and out. For some urban gardeners, containers may be the most suitable way to have trees. The good news is that many species will take well to containers. For ideas, take a look at the tree chart on page 102.

A tree's rooting space is limited in a container, so the larger the pot, the larger the tree you can grow. Planters, pots, and boxes of all sizes, shapes, and styles are sold in materials ranging from wood to plastic to terra-cotta. If you are considering moving or if you're gardening on a terrace or roof garden, weight and mobility are key factors pointing toward plastic pots, which are lightweight and durable. Larger built-in planters are a good choice if you are creating a permanent planting. Whatever size or style you choose, make sure the container has good drainage holes, holds enough soil for your tree, and will fit into the landscape well.

Give your tree a good soil mix that includes a variety of organic and inorganic compounds. Commonly used blends include pine bark, compost, sand, and expanded clay products. These blends require supplementation with a slow-release fertilizer with micronutrients at least once a year. One advantage of containers is that you can customize the soil to suit the tree you want to grow, which is not easy to achieve in a yard with existing soil and not good gardening practice anyway.

Good drainage is just as important as a good soil mix. Fill the bottom of the container with two to three inches of gravel or small rocks to allow water to move out through the drainage holes. If possible, elevate the container a few inches above the ground to give it enough room to drain.

Container-grown trees dry out rapidly because of their small rooting space, so you will need to water regularly, especially during the first year. As with most trees, it's best to give your container tree a thorough drenching each time you water. You may need to water daily as it grows bigger. Once it becomes root-bound, it should be root-pruned. To do this, remove the tree from its container and cut back its root ends using hand pruners. If your tree is too large to lift out, use a sharp digging spade to carefully dig a few inches in from the edge of the pot. Cut and remove roots and soil with your spade. When you are finished, replace the lost soil and water the pot right away. The best time to prune the roots is before bud break, or with tropical trees, before a new flush of growth.

Barbara Blechman, a New York City–based horticulturist, says that watering and good drainage are the most important maintenance tasks in containerized tree care. Root pruning and replacing the soil come next in importance. During the hotter months she sometimes adds extra fertilizer, since the higher temperatures and additional watering more rapidly deplete fertilizers.

To slow down top growth and root growth on deciduous trees, regularly prune back the tips of branches to buds along the stems. The tree will be less likely to make new sprouts if you prune just a little every year after the tree's spring growth spurt (after mid-June in most areas). Do not overprune or make heading cuts that will change the tree's natural shape. (See "Pruning Primer" on page 48 to familiarize yourself with proper pruning techniques.) I like to wait a season after root pruning before doing any major stem pruning to give the tree some time to recover and grow new roots. For coniferous trees, pinch out some of the new growth as it appears in spring.

There are a number of variables to consider when choosing trees for containers: planter size and location, available sunlight and water, and the plant's hardiness. Soil in a container will freeze before the soil in the ground, so root hardiness is very important when selecting a tree. Don't be afraid to try different types of trees, even if they don't make it—experimentation is what makes gardening fun.

**If you haven't enough space for a tree or want to keep it small, grow it in a container. This is also a great way to utilize a microclimate in your garden, for example, in a spot sheltered from the wind and warmed by the heat absorbed by surrounding walls.**

# Pruning Primer

Timing Choosing the right time for pruning is important for the health of your tree. The best season for most maintenance pruning is winter, when trees are dormant. The next best time is midsummer, when tree resources are at their highest for the year. It is wise to refrain from pruning between bud break and new leaf formation in spring and during leaf drop in fall, the periods when a tree's resources are at their lowest. The only exception from these guidelines is pruning deadwood and damaged branches and any pruning done for safety reasons, which can be done at any time of year.

Tools There are three tools I always use when I prune trees: a high-quality 13-inch pruning saw with a tri-cut blade for limbs up to 10 inches in diameter; a thinner, shorter saw with finer teeth for making smaller cuts and fitting between crowded limbs; and a pair of Felco #2 pruners, good all-around hand shears for pruning at the tips or cutting small branches. I never use loppers, machetes, or bow saws for pruning. They are difficult to use and don't make good finishing cuts at the branch collar. I find that with any tool you get what you pay for, so try to buy the best you can afford. The only ladder to use for pruning small trees or large shrubs is a tripod orchard ladder, made for tree pruning. They are sold in sizes up to 16 feet tall; a 10- or 12-footer works fine for most uses. Extension ladders or stepladders should never be used for pruning.

Safety Bear in mind that you'll be using sharp tools and that cut limbs suddenly released to gravity can be surprisingly heavy. Do not prune from a stepladder, do not use a chain saw, and always wear gloves and eye protection.

**Proper pruning makes or breaks a young tree and is vital for the continued well-being of mature trees. If you have a youngster like this *Acer griseum*, take care of structural problems early to avoid potential hazards later on. The most important pruning task for this tree is removing one of the two codominant stems at the top so that it can develop one strong leader.**

# Pruning Techniques

Thinning Cuts You will use thinning cuts for virtually all your tree pruning. Thinning cuts are used to direct and shape a tree's growth by establishing a strong basic structure. They can also promote good health by reducing foliage and letting in more light and air to the tree's interior.

Thinning cuts remove a branch back to another branch or to the trunk, leaving terminal buds intact on the remaining branches. (By contrast, a heading cut is made between buds and removes only the tip, resulting in a branch with many lateral buds but no terminal bud.)

When removing a branch, cut it all the way back to the area just outside the branch collar. The collar often appears as a swelling at the branch base, the area where a tree naturally sheds a dead branch. The branch collar is a natural protection zone within the tree that contains defensive chemicals and smaller water-conducting elements. The tree forms a chemical barrier against pathogens attempting to enter through the open pruning wound. The chemical barrier is made by phenols, which harden off and seal the wood, making it less appealing to bacteria and fungi. To limit the spread of disease and decay, trees also create a physical boundary to wall off the affected area. They build internal barriers within the wood to prevent infections from spreading. Cutting just outside the collar allows the tree to take full advantage of its natural defenses and protects the stem tissue from infection.

Making a good pruning cut right to the collar is

**Always use thinning cuts when you prune a tree. Thinning takes a branch back to another branch or to the trunk, preserving the natural architecture of the tree and promoting a strong growth pattern.**

called target or natural pruning. Your goal is to find the collar and prune just outside of it without leaving a stub. If you make a good cut, woundwood will form all around the cut end and slowly close up the injury.

Finding the branch collar is part of the art and craft of good pruning. Branch collars vary from tree to tree. On some species, especially those with thin bark and horizontal branching like beeches, maples, and magnolias, they are usually very obvious, but on others, particularly those with upright branches and thick bark, such as elms and most conifers, they are mostly inconspicuous. Even on a single tree you may find collars on some limbs and not on others. If you see collars on some branches but not on others, the branches without collars may be codominant stems, which contain no protection zone in their union and are best pruned out when the tree is small.

**Heading Cuts** Sometimes these cuts are also called heading back or internodal cutting, or when done on a larger scale, topping. No matter what it's called, never do this type of pruning unless you are trying to create a hedge of trees. A heading cut is made anywhere between the terminal bud and a branch union or the trunk. This cut removes the terminal bud, which has controlled all growth up to that point. All new growth will now be generated by lateral buds, which will start to sprout profusely. What is useful for thickening a hedge is absolutely wrong for grooming an individual tree.

**Never use heading cuts when you prune a tree. Heading destroys the natural growth pattern of the tree because it eliminates terminal buds and produces dangerous, weakly attached branches.**

## Bad for Trees: Heading Cuts

# The Three-Cut Technique

The weight of branches can be difficult to control during pruning. If they tear off, they can easily pull strips of bark off the trunk. Using a three-cut technique prevents such damage. It also allows you to carefully aim your final cut just outside the branch collar and branch bark ridge without having to contend with the weight of the branch.

Step 1 Notch the underside of the limb, cutting from the bottom toward the top. Make the cut 6 to 12 inches out from the trunk or branch collar from which the limb originates. Stop the cut before the saw binds.

Step 2 Start the next cut at the top of the branch, out 1 to 3 inches from the bottom notch, and saw all the way through the limb until it falls, if possible.

Step 3 Carefully remove the remaining stub, cutting just outside the branch collar (visible underneath the branch) and the branch bark ridge (a dark line that starts in the branch union).

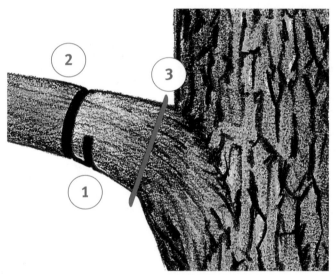

Cutting a notch on the underside of the branch prevents bark from ripping down the trunk in the event that the branch tears off. Use this technique every time you work with a pruning saw.

Don't rush the third step: The quality of your final cut determines whether or not the wound will close up properly over time. The size, angle, and shape of branch collars vary greatly from one species to the next. They also vary somewhat between trees of the same species—and even from one branch to another of the same tree. Consequently, the ideal angle for the cut that removes the stub just outside the branch collar will be different each time. The illustrations on the facing page represent some of the various branch unions and collars and are meant to help you determine the right places for cuts. If you are unsure about the correct position for your cut, also look for well-closed pruning cuts on other trees of the same species.

# How to Prune Branches Outside the Branch Collar

To remove a limb, cut it off just outside the branch collar and the branch bark ridge. Collars and bark ridges vary according to tree species and age. With luck, you'll see the collar on the branch underside and the ridge where trunk and branch tissue meet in the branch union. In each case, the dashed line indicates the correct pruning cut.

A and B: On some trees branch collars are obvious.

C: Trunks form large collars around the base of low, horizontal branches on some older trees, typically indicating a weak or dying limb.

D: When the branch collar is hard to see, draw an imagininary line that is parallel with the trunk and starts in the branch union. Estimate the angle between the line and the bark ridge (A). The angle of your pruning cut (B) is the same as angle A. The cut often ends at the same level as the end of the bark ridge.

E and F: Cut a branch forming a weak, V-shaped union with no collar or bark ridge so that the cut ends where branch and trunk tissue meet; it may be several inches (young tree) or feet (older tree) into the branch union. The cut may have to be finished with a chisel to limit injury of trunk tissue.

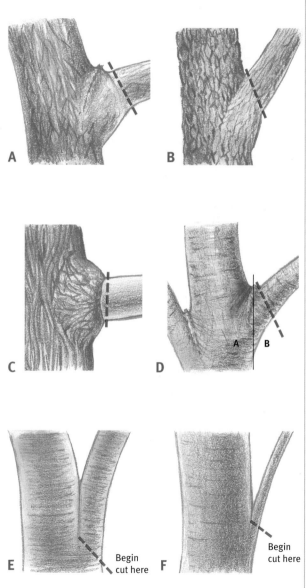

Properly done, a pruning cut leaves the branch collar intact. The collar region contains vital protective chemicals that help the tree to fight off infection. The collar also forms woundwood, which lends structural support and can close the pruning wound fully over time.

The lack of woundwood formation at the bottom of these old cuts indicates that the pruner removed part of the branch collar. This can lead to greater infection and make the tree more prone to wood rot.

## Of Flush Cuts and Wound Dressings

Not so long ago, pruning branches flush to the trunk (inside the branch collar), usually called a flush cut, was standard practice for gardeners and professional arborists alike. More recently, the flush cut has been proven to be very damaging for tree health. We now know that removing the branch collar leaves the trunk open to infection and decay. Alex Shigo, a tree biologist and former chief scientist for the U.S. Forest Service, spearheaded the research that led the trend away from flush cuts more than 20 years ago, but the harmful practice continues today. Shigo also found that wound dressings meant to protect the tree from wood rot often did more harm than good; by trapping moisture in the wound, dressing can actually stimulate decay.

## How Much Should You Prune?

Pruning trees is as much art as it is science. Coaxing out a tree's unique form through selected cuts as well as knowing how to carefully remove a limb to its branch collar is part of the craftsmanship of pruning. In addition, knowing how much leaf-bearing or live wood can be removed requires the understanding of how a tree uses and stores energy throughout the year and throughout its life.

How many living branches can be removed at one time without harming the tree? There is no simple answer that applies to all trees, or even to all trees of a particular species. Many gardening books and magazines recommend percentages such as a third or a quarter of the canopy. These numbers are meaningless without taking into account the species, life stage, time of year, and general health of each individual tree. A sapling may be pruned to the ground, removing 100 percent of the stem, and it will still sprout

up from the roots to start a new top. Conversely, I have been reluctant to remove even one live branch of an old, mature tree that has been showing signs of decline.

When live limbs are cut off, the tree loses not only leaves that produce food but also the energy that had been stored in the removed parts. In addition, the tree will have to expend energy to compartmentalize pruning cuts and grow new leaves and sprouts if too much was removed.

**Though it may not kill the tree outright, excessive pruning—like that done here to accommodate power lines—seriously compromises its life expectancy.**

# Trees in Their Formative Years

From the time they are seedlings until they develop mature characteristics such as strong lateral growth and full height and crown size, trees are considered to be in their formative years and are called juvenile (the human equivalent of childhood and adolescence). The length of the juvenile stage varies greatly from species to species: Sequoias can remain juvenile for a century; cherries are juvenile for a mere 20 years.

During their formative years, trees put much of their energy toward growth and toward respiration, the physiological process that fuels growth. They store less energy to get them through their annual dormancy phase than mature trees and also use less energy to build up their defenses against insects and diseases. As they mature, they begin to put energy into reproduction.

As a result, young trees grow faster than more mature trees, though growth rates vary considerably among different species. Young willows will sometimes add more than ten feet in a year. But even some slow-growing species like oaks can put on 12 to 18 inches in height in a season. Juvenile trees are not only getting taller quickly, they are also branching out. More branches mean more leaves; more leaves produce more energy; more energy leads to more growth.

From an evolutionary perspective, growing fast may well be the best way to beat out the competition in a forest environment. There doesn't seem to be much point in spending energy on defenses against pests and diseases if you're fighting just to get your head above the crowd.

**In its formative years, a tree like this red buckeye, *Aesculus pavia*, has plenty of energy and grows fast above and below ground. It has very little deadwood or dysfunctional tissue.**

**Portable drip-irrigation bags are handy for watering just-planted trees. Remove the bags in the fall of the first growing season.**

Below ground, there is a lot of activity as well. Roots are spreading rapidly, stabilizing the tree and allowing it to absorb more nutrients from the soil. You can check how well a recently planted tree is rooting in with a simple shake test. It's as easy as it sounds: Carefully shake the tree by its trunk. Look down to see if the ground is moving around the base of the tree. If it does, the tree is not yet rooted in. If the base looks stable and the ground remains firm, the tree has started to anchor itself in the new site. If your tree is not stable two years after planting, carefully dig around the root ball and check that the roots are not growing in a circular pattern. If they are, tease them outward and root prune.

## Water Requirements

Rapid growth above and below ground requires plenty of water, which makes adequate hydration especially important during a tree's first few seasons after planting. Supplemental watering is especially crucial during the summer months, but it may also be necessary during long dry periods in spring or autumn. If it hasn't rained at least one inch in any given week during the summer, give the tree a good drenching. The water should penetrate two feet into the soil—frequent light waterings only encourage roots to form close to the soil surface. Water slowly using a slow hose, sprinkler, water-filled garbage can with holes punched in the bottom, or portable drip-irrigation bag. (These bags, sometimes sold under the name Treegators, are often seen at the bases of trees in multiple plantings. Use one only during the tree's first growing season; keeping it on longer may encourage rot.) If the leaves start flagging (drooping) in drought conditions, water more often than once a week. Avoid overwatering, however; in waterlogged soil the roots cannot take up oxygen and may rot. If the top three inches of soil do not dry out in a day, stop watering.

## The Benefits of Mulching

The ideal model for the ground at the base of a tree is a forest floor, which is covered with dead leaves and other organic matter that gradually breaks down into the soil. To simulate the forest floor, keep a good organic mulch—ground wood chips, composted leaves, or in a pinch, bark chips (which don't contain many nutrients)—around the tree. Add new mulch at least once a year. Be careful not to overdo it, though: Apply a layer that's just a few inches thick and keep it well away from the trunk. Mulch piled up around the trunk (known as volcano mulching) is a bad—and unfortunately very common—practice. Too deep a layer of mulch can create an environment that allows harmful fungi and molds to form. Also, don't place weed matting, landscape fabric, or any other material beneath the mulch that might prevent it from enriching the soil as it decomposes. As the tree grows bigger, you may want to expand the ring of mulch around it to discourage people from walking over the root zone and compacting the soil. A mulch layer also keeps lawn mowers at a safe distance from the trunk.

## Pruning Young Trees for Good Structure

Pruning is one of the most important aspects of tree maintenance. Many problems can be corrected with small cuts that are made when a tree is still young and can recover quickly. A series of small, well-placed cuts can correct defects that might oth-

If a young tree doesn't have a leader, pick the strongest branch near the top, gently bend it upward, and attach a stake to it to train it vertically so that it can become the new leader. At the same time prune out any competing leader(s).

erwise result in early branch failure, and in the worst case, lead to the removal of a mature tree that has turned into a safety hazard.

## GET TO KNOW YOUR TREE

Before you reach for your saw and hand pruners, be sure you know your tree. If you are not familiar with the growth rate and typical mature size and spread of the species or cultivar, consult a reference book such as *The Manual of Woody Plants,* by Michael Dirr, or one of the other references listed on page 114, or locate a living, mature version of your tree and study it. When you understand how that type of tree grows naturally and what your youngster will look like in 20 or 30 years, you can much better visualize what kind of pruning it needs now and what it may require over the next few years.

## SET PRIORITIES

Give the young tree a few years to get established in its new spot before you start with structural pruning, and be sure to read the "Pruning Primer," starting on page 48, to familiarize yourself with the proper techniques for cutting tree limbs. Right after planting, remove only deadwood and any broken branches. In the following years

**Observe your newly planted tree carefully. Give it at least a year to get established before you start structural pruning cuts. Then, your first priority is to develop a strong leader.**

you will aim to remove codominant stems (competing leaders), crowded or crossing limbs, and deadwood. Start by focusing on the development of the young tree's top portion. If it is single-stemmed, as most trees are, it should have a single leader, or main stem. If the tree has competing leaders, choose the strongest one and prune out the others. If your tree was poorly pruned or topped by the nursery, it may not have an upright leader at all, just horizontal branches. In that case, you may have to train the most suitable upper limb to an upright position and make it the new leader.

Over time, thin out any other limbs growing in the way of the new leader. Then move down the trunk and take out any branches that cross or rub against others. Thin out crowded branches, leaving the healthiest branch or the one growing in the most desirable direction. (The desirable distance between branches depends on the tree species, so there's no general rule.) How do you decide which of two branches to take out? A branch growing at a steep angle (too close to the trunk) is a sign that it is weakly attached. Again, whether an angle is too steep depends on the species. Codominant stems and branches with narrow angles of attachment can develop weak unions. When they develop, water sprouts (vertical shoots) can also be weakly attached.

It's also useful to think ahead and remove any branches that will interfere with other plants or grow into walkways or over roads in future years. The juvenile stage

**Prune a little bit every year, removing weakly attached branches, crossing branches, and codominant stems. A neglected tree may end up like the bedraggled specimen on the right.**

During the formative stage, trees bounce back relatively easily when they lose leaves and branches. And pruning cuts made on trees the size of this young eastern redbud (*Cercis canadensis*) are also smaller, and less traumatic, than ones made on larger, older trees.

is also the best time in the tree's life to thin out branches to allow more sunlight to penetrate the canopy. Branches that are smaller or lower down on the tree will eventually be shaded out and lose their usefulness for the tree. Thin these out slowly over time. If you wait a few years you can prune them out once they have died without depriving the tree of any living wood. Be sure to keep the branches that retain the tree's natural form.

## CORRECT STRUCTURAL DEFECTS OVER TIME

Be patient. Step back often to look at the overall picture as you prune. The hardest part may be learning when to stop. Spread out pruning tasks over several years, removing a few branches each year rather than many at one time. Do the most important structural cuts first, then prune prudently until the tree reaches its early maturity. By that time you should have shaped the tree in such a way that it requires only minimal pruning of live wood as it gets older.

## OBSERVE HOW YOUR TREE RESPONDS TO PRUNING CUTS

There are no hard and fast rules about how much to prune at any one time. Without evaluating each individual tree, it's almost impossible to determine how much cutting is safe. The biology of each tree is different, and how much energy each one has stored away to help it through crises, including severe pruning, is also different. The best advice is to start small, then wait and see how the tree responds. The only exception is for hazardous branches or storm-damaged limbs, which should be removed as soon as you notice them.

Healthy juvenile trees take well to pruning. At this stage, trees have lots of energy for new growth and bounce back quickly. They are able to do this in part because the diameters of their trunks and limbs are smaller than those of older trees, and pruning cuts are smaller. The smaller the wound, the less chance there is of infection and long-term damage.

## Pruning for Safety

There are many benefits to pruning young trees as they develop, but do they really need it? Next time you take a walk in a forest, look up. You'll see that the first limbs on many large trees start about 50 feet up the tree. What happened to all the lower branches? Did they fall victim to the rarely seen translucent sawtail tree squirrel? Probably not. Trees are self-pruning: They naturally shed unproductive limbs. Trees use branches to extend their leaves as far as possible in order to absorb the maximum amount of sunlight. But branches can become shaded out or injured as the tree grows. Limbs that are unproductive become liabilities to the tree, so the tree has ways of naturally removing

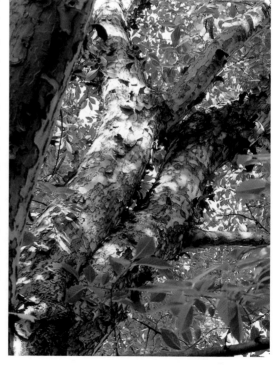

It's best to prune out problems like codominant stems when the tree is juvenile: On a mature tree they can create health and safety issues for both the tree and you.

them. If trees are self-pruning, why do we gardeners need to prune? One reason is that we plant trees around our homes, parks, and roadways, and we don't want to be under a tree when it sheds that unwanted branch.

There are a few other reasons, too. Trees planted in the human landscape tend to have more space than trees in the forest. Because they are not crowded by competing trees, their lower limbs are rarely shaded out. Arborists call these trees "open grown." An open-grown tree can develop much larger scaffold branches, which become permanent structural branches of the tree. This can give you a picturesque, beautifully spreading shade tree or a time bomb with vulnerable codominant stems and weak branch attachments. Pruning the tree when it's young is the best way to avoid these problems down the road.

## Protecting Young Trees From Deer

Young trees are vulnerable to two kinds of deer damage: injury to lower limbs as deer nibble off leaves, buds, and fruit within their reach, and bark damage as bucks rub their antlers against the trunks in fall and early winter to leave their scent and remove the velvet from their developing antlers. Tree branches that are lower than about five feet from the ground are susceptible to deer foraging. Trunks that are under four inches in diameter and that still have smooth, immature bark are preferred by bucks.

To prevent browsing in the lower branches, fence young trees. Drive three or four tall wooden stakes into the ground around each tree, about 48 inches from the trunk, and attach chicken wire or heavy plastic mesh to the stakes to form an enclosure all the way around the tree. To protect the trunks of smaller trees from buck rub-

**The bark of this young tree was severely—perhaps mortally—damaged when a buck rubbed its antlers against it in fall or early winter.**

bing, enclose the trunk with a plastic trunk protector, which is available in several forms. You can also make your own trunk protector: Purchase a length of perforated PVC pipe wide enough to fit loosely around the tree's trunk. Cut a slit down its length with a utility knife, pry it open, and slide it around the trunk. A more airy option is galvanized wire mesh loosely wrapped around the tree trunk. Check trunk protectors regularly. Excess heat or moisture can accumulate inside the plastic ones, causing cracked or split bark, fungal and bacterial diseases, borer infestations, and cambial damage. And if any trunk protector gets too tight, it can restrict plant growth and severely compromise the bark.

If you don't have a dog or two to frolic around the yard—probably the best deer deterrent—you can try repellents, which usually repulse deer by either taste or odor. Many repellents are now available in garden centers, or you can make your own home-made repellent by mixing one egg, one cup milk, one tablespoon cooking oil, and one tablespoon dish soap into one gallon of water. It's best to apply repellents in early spring before bud break and new growth appears, and before deer establish a feeding pattern. Apply every three to four weeks, alternating products so that the deer don't become used to a particular repellent, and reapply after heavy rains. Strongly scented soap bars can also work—some gardeners recommend hanging several, still in their wrappers so they don't disintegrate too quickly, from the lower branches of vulnerable trees. Visual and aural deterrents, such as dangling tin-foil pie pans, ribbon stream-ers, and wind chimes are also rec-ommended by many gardeners, although as with the other repel-lents, they should be rotated periodically to keep the deer spooked.

**To prevent bucks from damaging the bark of a young tree, enclose the trunk using perforated PVC pipe or galvanized wire mesh, as shown here, or buy a ready-made protector.**

## Street Trees

Originally, street trees were planted in cities and towns not to shade people from the summer sun but to keep workhorses comfortable. To this day, city street trees are commonly spaced about 23 feet apart, the standard distance between two horses tied up along the curb. Today we value our urban forest for the cool shade and beauty it offers and also for the trees' ability to reduce air and noise pollution, mitigate storm-water runoff, and improve property values. Overall, the presence of trees makes for a much more pleasant neighborhood.

Street trees may be the most challenging of all landscape plantings, however. A city street or suburban roadside can be a hostile environment for a tree. The worst problem is the compaction of soils under pavement, which severely compromises a tree's root development. Salts and chemicals that help in snow and ice removal further harm tree roots. Urine from too many dogs visiting the same tree can also hurt roots. Leaves can be scorched or damaged by heat reflected from pavements and buildings. Street trees are often overpruned for road clearance and power lines. Their trunks are easily damaged by bumpers from parking vehicles, and their limbs are broken by large trucks. Many trees die within a few years of planting because they were not planted properly and didn't receive adequate water while they were getting established. In a survey conducted by the conservation organization American Forests, city street trees were found to have a life expectancy of only seven to ten years.

A few species and hybrids such as elms (*Ulmus* species), London plane (*Platanus* × *acerifolia*), and maples (*Acer* species) that can survive in harsh conditions and can make do with little water, have emerged as favorites in North American cities. But reliance on just a few trees brings the dangers inherent in monoculture: Large

Often seen on street trees, girdling roots are very harmful. Wrapping around the base, they strangle the tree and compromise its ability to absorb water. These roots should have been removed when the tree was planted.

numbers of trees can be killed in a short time when an insect or a disease outbreak comes sweeping through the neighborhood. Dutch elm disease is a telling example: In less than 80 years it has killed millions of elms across the continent and left many cities and towns devoid of street trees.

Most urban foresters now favor more diversified plantings to reduce the chances of rapid spread if a disease or pest outbreak occurs. Work done by Nina Bassuk of Cornell University and others has focused on identifying new ways to improve the chances for newly planted street trees to become established. Part of their effort has been to evaluate many never-tried species as street trees. They also tested a structural soil mix that is load bearing and suitable for use under pavements and also better for tree-root growth than unmodified soil. Known as CU-Soil, the mixture is composed of a stone-on-stone lattice for strength, with soil and pore space between the stones. This new soil mix is designed for use under sidewalks, parking lots, or other areas where trees are planted in pavement. The cost of installing structural soil is higher than conventional methods, but in the long term, since CU-Soil improves tree health and longevity, it saves money otherwise spent on tree replacement and other care.

## Taking Care of Street Trees

Though it is true that most trees planted outside of their natural settings need some special consideration, young roadside and urban street trees need serious attention if they are to survive and thrive.

Water is the number one requirement for young street trees to get established. Apply 15 to 20 gallons of water slowly once a week from spring to fall unless it rains at least one inch per week.

Spread two to three inches of good organic mulch around the base of the tree, but keep it several inches away from the trunk to avoid volcano mulching.

Apply compost tea (see page 106 for more information).

Begin pruning the tree once it's established (two to three years after planting). Remove smaller branches that are growing low on the tree and develop a strong central leader. Note: Check with civic authorities before making any pruning cuts or other permanent adjustments; you might need a permit or pruning certificate.

Plant groundcovers and flowers in the tree pits. They beautify the sidewalk and signal to passersby that the tree is cared for and respected. Tree pit plantings are also a useful reminder to water the tree.

Remove anything tied around the tree like signs or tags right away. Be sure to remove any staking wires or ties after one growing season.

Be an advocate for trees in your city or town.

# Early Mature and Mature Trees

Mature trees have attained their full ornamental potential: They produce flowers and fruit, and if they are deciduous they often display wonderful fall color. As trees reach their mature size and shape, growth starts slowing down. At the same time, their static mass—the dysfunctional or dead tissue (also called false heartwood and protection wood) found at the innermost part of the tree in the trunk and branches—increases. The static mass provides structural support for the tree but does not contribute to building energy reserves for the tree. At this stage in their lives, trees in their natural forest environment may have as much deadwood as live branches. They often have wounds, decayed parts, and sometimes hollow areas in the trunks. Mature trees in an urban or suburban setting may have had many branches pruned off.

You can often tell whether a tree has reached maturity by comparing its size with the maximum size for its species and by looking at its general shape. A 75-foot-tall red oak (*Quercus rubra*), for example, is within the range of the species' maximum size—60 to 80 feet in height. The growth habit of a mature tree, reflected in its shape, is different from that of a juvenile. It no longer displays apical dominance. Instead, lateral buds grow more relative to apical buds, making a mature tree's growth spread more evenly. In consequence, the canopy of a mature tree is likely to be flatter at the top and more rounded overall.

A mature tree has to spend a lot of energy just to maintain its mass. It also spends a larger percentage of its resources on reproduction and defense than a juvenile tree does.

**A mature tree like this Japanese tree lilac, *Syringa reticulata*, has reached its full crown size. Growth slows down and becomes more outward and lateral than upright at this stage in life.**

It makes enough food to support all these processes but does not have the same level of energy reserves as a juvenile tree. Nevertheless, even through bad years when it is subjected to drought, pests, or root damage, it can continue at this level for a long time.

## Water Needs and Mulching

Healthy mature trees should have adapted to the conditions at their site. For this reason most do not need supplemental watering unless there is a drought. Even then, trees that are not used to it can be damaged by the extra watering, which can cause root rot. Trees such as white oak (*Quercus alba*) that have evolved in arid environmental niches are especially sensitive to the effects of additional watering. Water trees only if they show signs of flagging (drooping leaves). If you have to water, provide a good thorough soaking once a week rather than more frequent light waterings.

Maintain a layer of mulch two to three inches thick around your mature tree's trunk, as far out toward the drip line as you can, but keep it several inches away from the trunk itself. Use a good organic mulch of wood chips or composted leaves: Organic mulch is far better than any plant fertilizer you can buy. It breaks down slowly, improving soil structure and protecting the tree's root zone. I find that occasional drenches of compost tea are also beneficial. (See "Tree Health Care," page 104, for more information.)

## Minimizing the Effects of Change

Keeping a mature tree healthy is mostly a matter of protecting it and its surrounding environment from change. A tree's root zone can easily extend up to twice the diameter of the drip line of the canopy, making it very vulnerable to damage below ground. If there are groundcovers, turf, or other plants already growing under an old tree, it has probably adapted to them, but any new changes to the landscape around it should be made with great care and slowly over time if possible. Avoid digging or changing the grade of the soil: Digging even a foot deep near a tree can greatly damage its roots since most of them lie in this shallow zone. Adding soil or too deep a layer of mulch under the tree can likewise hurt roots, suffocating them or leading to other health problems.

Many more mature trees fall victim to home- and landscape-improvement projects than to insects or diseases. Rototilling, sidewalk and driveway repair, trenching for lawn sprinklers, and other gardening projects can do great damage to trees and their root systems. Other sudden changes to the tree's environment, like fertilizing, soil

**Minimal intervention is essential for the long-term health of a mature tree. This applies to the tree itself as well as its immediate surroundings. Though low-growing branches are usually removed, it is not necessary to do so if a beautifully growing limb is not in the way.**

compaction, overpruning, wounding the trunk or roots, and even removing other trees around it can also be harmful—and perhaps trigger the decline of a mature tree.

Construction One of the biggest killers of trees in urban areas is damage from construction. The most serious damage is caused by digging, trenching, and soil compaction by construction equipment rather than by branches being broken or split. Trees are rooted in place and can't get out of the way, so we must guard mature trees against this kind of damage. Before you undertake any construction that may affect your trees, devise a tree-protection plan. If heavy equipment will be used, fence off as much of the area around your tree's root zone as possible. You can consult an arborist about how to minimize the damage to your trees during construction.

Changes in Grade Adding soil on top of the root system of trees—especially species in temperate zones whose roots are close to the soil surface—can reduce the amount of air in the root zone and may even suffocate roots. By changing the grade around a tree, you might increase the depth of the soil atop the roots and/or change the way water flows over the area, increasing moisture in places that were somewhat dry, or vice versa. If you must add soil to the area around a tree, try to keep it as far from the trunk as possible. One way to increase the flow of oxygen through the soil is having a contractor insert small-diameter perforated PVC pipes horizontally or vertically through the additional soil; fill these pipes with gravel or leave them empty. Be sure to keep a record of their positions—you may want to refer to it during future projects.

**Gardening Beneath Mature Trees** Many gardeners have conflicting feelings about their older trees. They love their beauty and grace but are less thrilled by the dense shade and the limitations that a large root zone imposes. The aesthetic ambition to have a tree or two in a garden setting can easily come into conflict with the trees' biological needs. Arborists are often asked to thin a tree to allow more light to fall onto the lawn and garden. But pruning live wood at this stage of development will seriously affect the tree's energy balance. There are pretty good reasons why the tree has matured to its current shape. Its form at this stage is the result of a lifetime of adjusting its growth to the world around it.

Planting a variety of shade-tolerant species underneath a mature tree is a much better

solution than thinning out branches for more light. There are many plants to choose from that grow naturally in the vicinity of trees and have similar water, soil pH, and general cultural needs. Choose plants that are compatible with the growing conditions of your tree and grow well in shade; woodland bulbs, groundcovers, perennials, as well as small shrubs that are native in your area are excellent choices for many types of deciduous trees.

**Add visual interest and limit foot traffic with shade-loving plants that are compatible with the conditions under a mature tree and don't compete with its root system.**

When making your selections, choose small plants and don't dig your planting holes too deeply or too close to the trunk. If the new plants like their growing conditions, their root systems will gradually and naturally become incorporated with the area around the tree's root zone. Avoid plants that will compete with the tree's root system for nutrients and moisture, such as ivy (*Hedera helix*). Remember that most trees have very wide but shallow root systems that are easily damaged. Never rototill or add soil over the top of the root zone when planting.

A large vine growing up into a tree's canopy burdens it with substantial extra weight and shades out its leaves. It may also camouflage potentially hazardous conditions.

**Vines and Trees** Keep vines from growing rampantly up into both young and mature trees. Vines can become heavy, and their weight may be harmful to a tree—they may even eventually strangle or girdle it. As vines grow up among the foliage, they can also compete with the tree's leaves for sunlight. Underneath their lush foliage, vines may also hide a tree's health problems, like decaying wood. An annual vine growing up the trunk of an older tree or a perennial vine growing partway up the trunk shouldn't be a problem, but trim back all vines each year to keep them safely out of the tree's canopy.

## Using Fertilizers With Care

Often recommended by tree or lawn services and landscaping firms, tree fertilization is big business—and often a big mistake. The only reason to fertilize a tree is if it is deficient in a specific soil nutrient. Trees signal nutrient deficiencies by producing discolored leaves or stunted growth. If your tree is showing any of these signs, have the soil analyzed and consult an arborist, who can recommend organic soil remedies. Use fertilizers only if recommended to address a specific soil problem. Applying fertilizer unnecessarily or in too large quantities is bad for the environment as a whole and can be very harmful to your tree and the soil organisms that aerate the soil and promote root development and absorption of water and nutrients.

Fertilizers are often marketed and sold as "plant food," which is a clever marketing ploy to make us think they are necessary and beneficial. The truth is that plants produce their own food through photosynthesis, and that's the only way they get energy. You can't pour a bag of energy into the soil. Fertilizers can stimulate plant growth, but the plant pays for that growth from its own energy stores.

A mature tree that's doused with a fertilizer high in nitrogen is forced to grow and may use up valuable resources it needs for defense and other functions, leaving it more vulnerable to insect and disease damage. Ironically, the same tree or lawn service that insists you need to fertilize your trees will happily spray your tree for any infestation that the fertilizer treatment may promote. Avoid this vicious circle. Instead of applying fertilizer, focus on preventing stressful conditions and supplying your trees with good-quality organic mulches and compost.

## Pruning Mature Trees

Pruning mature trees is about managing the safety of the tree rather than changing its shape. Mature trees need as many leaves as possible so that they can produce the maximum amount of food. At this stage, trees really need to build up their energy reserves, so the pruning of live wood should be kept to a minimum.

Mature trees need to be periodically inspected for deadwood, damaged or weak branches, and potentially hazardous defects in their structure. A professional arborist or tree consultant should do this type of inspection, because it may be necessary to go up into the canopy to look closely at the branches and leaves. Pruning a large tree can be dangerous work and shouldn't be attempted by a homeowner—even one who just bought a new chain saw. Homeowners who have leaned a ladder up against a large tree and attempted to remove large branches have been killed in the process. Qualified arborists use ropes and harnesses for their own safety and can remove branches without damaging the tree or nearby property.

Less skilled pruners who attach to their boots climbing spikes like those used by utility workers to climb telephone poles will harm the tree. The spikes puncture the bark and leave holes that can lead to infection. Another common technique people use to work in large trees is an aerial lift mounted on a truck. This is fine as long as

**During its long life, a landscape tree may experience neglect, sustaining broken limbs and developing defects like crossing and wayward branches, as well as sprouts. Pruning should be limited to removing hazards and careful cuts to promote the longevity of the tree.**

the truck remains on a paved area or outside the tree's drip line. If the truck drives over a tree's root zone, it can severely compact the soil and cause root damage.

## Hiring an Arborist

Arborists are people who have studied the art and science of planting, pruning, and caring for trees. When you decide it's time to hire a professional tree-care company, look for a person or company with whom you will develop an ongoing relationship. Talk to several prospects and find out about their overall approach: Do they practice preventive health care or integrated pest management? (See page 105.) What techniques would they use to care for the beautiful old tree that's next to your house? Steer away from companies that suggest topping a tree or removing an excessive amount of live wood. Also avoid people who use climbing spikes on trees that are not being removed.

Pruning sprouts, left, is one of the few tasks you should attempt yourself. Any pruning that involves climbing into a mature tree and operating a chain saw should be done by a qualified arborist, who can remove a large branch without harming the tree or anything else.

Ask about and check on the credentials of the companies you interview: Are they members of and certified by a professional tree-care organization such as the International Society of Arboriculture (ISA), the Tree Care Industry Association (TCIA), or the American Society of Consulting Arborists (ASCA)? Does your state require licensing of arborists, and if so, is the arborist licensed? Ask for proof that the company carries liability insurance for personal and property damage and workman's compensation. Ask for references and check their work on nearby properties. Make sure that the people who will be doing the work are as qualified as the person you meet with initially; ideally this is the person who will do or oversee the work. Be suspicious if an arborist is willing to lower his or her prices to get the job.

If your municipality requires permits for tree work, make sure that the arborist applies for and receives one. Most reputable arborists ask their clients to sign a contract before starting the work. Be sure to read this contract carefully, and make sure it includes the work to be done, the dates on which the work will be started and completed, the party responsible for cleanup, and the total cost of the work.

It's very helpful to educate yourself on some of the basic principles of tree care before hiring an arborist. If you have questions that go beyond the scope of this book, consult some of the references listed on page 114, or talk to your local garden center, cooperative extension agent, or city arborist. Trees that are cared for improperly may not recover for years, if ever.

## Stop Topping!

Topping—making a heading cut to a large branch of a mature tree—is a bad idea that's surprisingly popular. When a tree is topped, it tends to generate very vigorous, suckery new branches where the cuts were made. They may eventually extend their spindly growth back to the former full height of the tree, but these new branches are weakly attached to the stem and prone to breakage. Another problem is that a branch that's cut off mid-limb lacks natural protection; it cannot compartmentalize and contain infection, making the cut end an open invitation to disease and pest problems. A flush of branching in an area of advancing decay is another ingredient in this recipe for future failure.

**Topping destroys the beauty of a tree and should never be done. If a tree's canopy poses a safety risk, consult a qualified arborist. If there are no viable pruning options, have the entire tree removed.**

Topping also removes large branches whose foliage has been generating energy for the root system. The tree's roots will receive less food, and some will die off, resulting in a loss of stability. If you have a mature tree that may pose safety problems, have it evaluated by a qualified arborist. He or she may suggest other methods to make the tree safe or propose that it's better to remove the tree altogether.

# Trees, Neighbors, Money, and the Law

Years ago, I had some clients who had a beautiful, mature red maple in their small Brooklyn, New York, backyard. They had planted it the first spring after they moved in 50 years earlier and had cared for it well. Needless to say, they were quite attached to this tree. Over time the maple's trunk, roots, and many branches had grown into the property of neighbors who loved the tree too, and sat in its shade and looked forward to its fall color.

The tree was in good condition when the owners called me initially for a consultation, and I told them to get back in touch in three years. A year later my client called, almost in tears. New neighbors had moved in. They thought such a big tree was unsafe, and they didn't want to have to clean up its leaves in fall. They wanted the tree cut down. I talked to the new neighbors, but they had made up their minds, and when my client next called I could hear the chain saw in the background. The neighbors had the portions of the tree removed that were hanging over their property. This amounted to about half the tree, damaging it so much that the rest of it had to be removed soon after.

My clients decided to sue, so we contacted a member of the American Society of Consulting Arborists to determine the tree's dollar value. To determine the value of a tree, the ASCA, which specializes in plant appraisal, uses a formula that is recognized by most U.S. courts. Called the "trunk formula method" (TFM), it is based on the trunk size, the tree's condition before the damage, its location, species, and a few other factors. Using this formula, a 15-inch-diameter (measured at breast height) sugar maple on a New England street could be valued at $4,500 to $6,000. The maple in my client's backyard, at over 30 inches in diameter, was worth some serious money. The neighbors settled out of court, and we planted a fast-growing dawn redwood, which grows tall but not wide. I don't think the couples talk to each other to this day.

The number one reason that homeowners cut down or top their trees—often perfectly healthy trees like this one—is that they are afraid of the damage trees or their limbs will do if they fall. Even if you know your trees are healthy and safe, your neighbor may not believe this to be the case. To protect your trees there are a few things you should know.

Laws all over North America are becoming increasingly protective of trees, with many localities now requiring tree removal permits. Be sure you know the local laws and ordinances.

The trees on your property are your responsibility, and you may be liable if one falls and injures someone. But—and this is the important part—you are only liable if you knew or should have known that a tree posed a hazard. A tree with a big dead limb hanging over a sidewalk is an obvious hazard. But some defects may be inside the tree's wood or roots and not visible. And if a tree or its branches fall because of a tornado, lightning, or ice storm, you probably will not be liable. The best way to

**It pays to have large trees like this imposing evergreen inspected regularly. If a tree on your property falls, you may be liable if you should have known it posed a hazard.**

protect your trees and yourself is to have your bigger trees regularly cared for by a professional arborist.

Trees growing on property lines are considered jointly owned in most states. Most local ordinances give a neighbor the right to trim the tree or shrub back to the property line. However, legal decisions in California and elsewhere recently held that a neighbor cannot unreasonably damage the health of a tree by pruning it back. Fallen leaves, fruit, even small branches that end up on a neighbor's property are considered a natural occurrence, and you are not responsible for cleaning them up.

Disputes between neighbors can also arise when trees block views. Because property values are often linked to good views, neighbors may be inclined to sue to get a tree removed. Some subdivisions have undertaken "view zoning," prohibiting the planting of large tree species in "viewsheds," in an attempt to preserve vistas. Unless your community has put this kind of ordinance in place, your neighbors will have a hard time forcing you to remove a tree. If a neighbor requests that you remove a tree and you're prepared to go along, the neighbor should pay for its removal. You may even have the tree appraised and ask for compensation. Of course, you can always inform complaining neighbors about how beneficial trees are for the neighborhood as a whole.

# Ancient Trees

Over time, mature trees slowly move into the last phase of their life span, what biologists call the ancient stage of tree life. From the human point of view, this is when trees develop real character: Their branches have become gnarled, and they may have developed a unique overall shape. During this stage trees go through a process called retrenchment. The canopy becomes more compact as the crown dies back, and the tree begins to shed large branches. Ancient trees show more signs of decline than of growth. They are less able than younger trees to form woundwood when they have been injured, and they put on less new growth after insect attacks or pruning. A tree that has lived a hard life, suffering from bad pruning, root damage, drought, and other stresses, will reach the ancient stage prematurely.

Trees can become their most hazardous to humans at this stage. Unsound branches can drop unexpectedly, or the trunk structure may fail. Reduction and safety pruning, root care, and integrated pest management (IPM) are the basic elements of care for trees that have reached the veteran stage.

Despite extensive decay and dieback, ancient trees can still be healthy and vigorous. Because their growth rate is significantly reduced, trees in this stage save a lot of energy. This may be why some trees can live a long time in this phase. The art of bonsai works on this principle. Trees planted as bonsai are greatly reduced by being pruned and installed in small pots, and they use little energy for growth. One goal of bonsai growers is to create a tree that looks like a veteran without having to wait hundreds of years.

**Ancient trees like this bristlecone pine, *Pinus aristata,* have low energy reserves because their leaf area declines as their crowns die back and they lose branches to damage and decay. Yet it is this continuous "downsizing" that allows them to live for thousands of years.**

Trees in the later ancient phase are described as being in terminal decline or in the senescent phase. At this stage they have large amounts of deadwood and are losing their crowns and root systems. They have reached the final phase of their life and spend the majority of their energy just to maintain themselves, which makes them more vulnerable to injury and pests. Over the course of decades—or possibly overnight—senescent trees can split apart or exhaust all of their energy stores. Some trees, like oaks, ginkgos, and redwoods, take many years to move from the early ancient phase to the senescent phase. For others, like cherries, willows, and some maple species, this transition may take only a few years. Still, some trees can remain in the ancient stage for a long time. In the 1950s, Edmund Schulman, a dendrochronologist (a scientist who studies climatic change through the growth rings of trees or old timber) at the University of Arizona, discovered the oldest living organisms in the world—bristlecone pines more than 4,000 years old. These small, gnarly trees grow in the harsh mountain environment of California's White Mountains at altitudes higher than 11,000 feet. Many of these trees are still alive today and are great attractions for nature

lovers. Other long-lived ancient trees are the old-growth redwoods of California and Sitka spruces from the Pacific Northwest, some of which are more than 2,000 years old. In Britain there are 1,000-year-old yews and 300- to 400-year-old oaks; in Japan there are ginkgos known to be centuries old.

A common misconception is that any tree discovered to be dying should be removed right away, especially if it appears hazardous or doesn't fit in with the gardening scheme of the moment. But even if they are not conven-

**Ancient trees are often beautiful and offer habitat for wildlife. Consider removing a veteran only if it is unsafe and may cause harm should it fail.**

tionally beautiful or valuable sources of timber, ancient trees play an important role as habitat for wildlife and as food for all kinds of other living organisms. If a declining tree is not endangering people or buildings and can be safely maintained, it can remain useful for years. A declining tree can also be very attractive in its own way, and observing it can be quite educational. You'll see birds, mushrooms, insects, and other small animals using the tree in various ways.

A resistograph measures the resistance to a thin needle inserted into wood. Used to diagnose defects and decay, it delivers accurate information about the health of a tree's wood while causing minimal damage.

Few trees growing in urban and suburban areas are allowed to reach the ancient stage. Most are removed when they start to drop large limbs or show signs of decay in their branches, trunk, or root system and begin to pose a hazard to humans and their homes. A few ancient trees that live alongside people do escape the ax, though. Most of these are found in open spaces and are valued as champions for their size or have historic or aesthetic value. A few of them have even become tourist attractions. Near Charleston, South Carolina, you can visit a live oak (*Quercus virginiana*), called the Angel Oak, that is approximately 1,400 years old. It is thought to be one of the oldest living organisms east of the Mississippi River. Its longest branch is 89 feet long.

Gardeners in Great Britain originated the term "veteran trees" to describe mature or ancient trees that have historic, aesthetic, or horticultural value. Many veteran trees are not hundreds of years old, just older than most members of their species and appreciated as valuable members of their community.

## Basic Care for Ancient Trees

Maintaining a veteran tree can be a serious—and sometimes expensive—commitment. Continue to add mulch each year around the base of the tree, covering as much of

This view of a tree from above shows a large hollowed-out limb where the trunk precariously branches three ways. This close to a building (and people), safety comes first: The hollow limb will be removed and the remaining leaders will be cabled together.

the area under the drip line as possible. Have the whole canopy and root system inspected by a qualified tree consultant every year. The outlook can be very different for trees that have matured to this stage naturally than for those that reached this stage prematurely through induced stress. Trees that have endured hard pruning or topping, severe storm damage, wounding, or pest and disease infestations may be more difficult to maintain and keep safe.

Safety should be the first priority when maintaining a veteran tree. Trees growing in sites where they could injure people or damage property or other valuable trees or plantings are not good candidates for this type of maintenance. In some cases, people build walls or fences around an important or historic tree to protect it from people—and people from the tree. The best management for a veteran tree is damage control. The first thing to do is make sure that the tree is not a hazard: You don't want branches falling on anyone or anything. Ensure that the root system is strong enough to keep the tree anchored, and keep the tree well mulched and watered. Remove any dead branches as they develop. Some older trees may need mechanical supports like braces or cabling.

# Hazardous Trees

What makes a tree hazardous? A potential victim: You, your house, passersby, nearby parked cars. An old-growth tree in the forest can simply live out its life, fall, and provide food and shelter for wildlife as it decays. But you are responsible for the tree in your yard, so you want to keep it structurally sound.

If your tree is downsizing and you are weighing whether to cut it down or extend its life with extraordinary measures, the first step is to get an evaluation by a professional arborist who specializes in hazard tree evaluations. An arborist looks for any "body language" that points to structural defects undermining the tree: cracks, wood decay, weak branching, deadwood, or a weak root system. Some of these might be obvious, but other indicators might be in the interior of the tree and not directly visible. Arborists use specialized instruments like resistographs and other minimally invasive diagnostic tools to help them determine the amount of decay or other defects in the wood. It is very difficult to predict if or when a branch or tree will fall. The arborist assigns categories of risk to a tree and determines whether there are ways to make it safe and how.

**Fungal growths such as this hen-of-the-woods mushroom are an indicator of dead spots on a trunk or branches and may signal trouble. Look for this tasty tidbit in fall.**

## Recognizing Defects

Injuries and decay can occur at any stage in a tree's life. But as a tree becomes older and larger, any defect becomes more problematic.

Trees cannot heal injured or decayed tissue. They can contain infection through compartmentalization, an ability that is stronger in some species than in others and diminishes with age.

Decay A big myth about trees is that they can heal their wounds. In fact, trees cannot replace or repair injured tissue as humans can. They do have the ability to stop infection from spreading through the wood by compartmentalization—containing the infection through the use of protective chemical and physical barriers. In a very old or very weak tree, this process may not be very efficient. In addition, some tree species are less effective at this than others, regardless of their age. The infection can continue to spread and cause structural weakness, sometimes visible as a sunken or hollow area in the trunk or a major branch. Fungal growth on the trunk or branches indicates dead spots in the wood. If a tree is home to carpenter ants, it probably has some decaying wood. In small numbers, carpenter ants can actually be beneficial to a tree, clearing out decayed wood and helping to stop the spread of infection. A large population of carpenter ants in a tree is now thought to be harmful, however; they may begin to chew through living wood. If a third of the outer part of the wood is sound, the tree can still be viable. But if a tree has more than two thirds decayed interior wood, it is unlikely to be structurally sound.

Cracks in a tree's wood are bad news. They can result from storm damage, bad pruning, or wounding—when a passing truck rips a limb from a tree, for example. Limbs with cracks should usually be removed. Cracks in the trunk can indicate serious defects.

Interestingly, depending on the number and orientation of cracks, they may balance each other. A single crack is a problem, and two cracks on opposite sides of a trunk are very serious, since they can cause the trunk to shear or split. But multiple cracks around a trunk can indicate that the tree has compensated and is structurally sound. Nevertheless, it should be evaluated.

**Root problems** Sometimes very hard to diagnose, root rot may be indicated by dieback at the tips of branches or by mushrooms or other fungal growth at the base of the tree. Digging in the root zone is a major cause of root damage, though it may not be evident for many years. Root failure can be very dangerous. If one of your trees shows signs of root problems, it should be looked at by a professional.

## Safety and Reduction Pruning

Older trees need special care when it comes to pruning because their energy reserves are small. Unless an elderly tree is hazardous and requires emergency treatment, it

**To promote the longevity of a veteran tree, develop a long-term pruning plan with an arborist. The first step is to examine the tree's basic structure with the goal of reducing the height and width of the crown over time. This helps to lighten the load that large scaffold limbs carry.**

Trees of advanced age naturally downsize. Crown-reduction pruning controls that process without harming the tree. First dead and hazardous branches are removed. Then lateral branches are thinned out at the tips. Done properly, this encourages new interior growth.

should be pruned back very slowly. Quickly removing large amounts of wood can push a veteran over the edge and into decline.

If you have a veteran tree, you should have it inspected for hazards and commit to a long-term pruning plan with an arborist. When I discuss veteran tree care with clients, I tell them that we are trying to manage the natural downsizing of the tree. This type of pruning is called crown reduction and should only be done when necessary and recommended by a qualified arborist. Crown-reduction pruning reduces the height and width of the canopy, encouraging new interior growth. Upright branches are pruned back to lower laterals that are at least half the size in diameter. Lateral branches can also be thinned at the tips to reduce their weight.

The first step is to remove dead and unsafe parts of the tree. Then, over the next five to ten years, the arborist should slowly reduce the canopy, using target pruning to make thinning cuts. An arborist should aim to prune back just enough of the weak structure over time to make the tree safe.

Popular with some tree services, "lion-tailing" is devastating for the health of a mature tree. In this approach, branches are removed from the interior. This promotes sprouting at the tips and adds weight to the structurally weakest areas—exactly where it should be lightened.

There may be cases, though, when an arborist must make a large heading cut as a last resort. When a large branch has become dangerously weakened and is growing directly over a house or walkway, it may be necessary to cut it off mid-limb rather than at a branch union. Before opting to remove such a limb, consider mechanically supporting it. For safety reasons the arborist may also have to head back part or all of an injured branch. Because the limbs on veteran trees can be so large, the tree is often unable to support a limb that has been injured. But pruning it out reduces the tree's ability to grow leaves and photosynthesize and can have a negative impact on the tree's longevity. Therefore, any large cuts on veteran trees must be very carefully considered.

Make sure that your arborist does not use "lion-tailing," a practice in which the interior of a branch is thinned and the tip area is left untouched. Pruners do this sometimes because it is easier for them, but it is very detrimental to the tree. Some interior pruning cuts may be large and over time lead to the decay of the remaining stems. Excessive weight can also develop from new shoot growth, making a lion-tailed limb more prone to failure because the remaining leaves are all at the tips.

Trees that compartmentalize well and that can send out new growth on old wood tend to respond well to reduction pruning. Examples include oaks, sycamores, and figs. You should see new growth the following year along with woundwood formation. If instead you see more dieback and no woundwood, the tree may be depleted and without the reserves to respond to the pruning. You may have to remove the tree or cut it back hard and leave it as a habitat tree (see page 95).

Timing is important when you undertake reduction pruning. If the tree poses a safety problem, attend to it right away. Otherwise, prune before the spring flush of growth if you want to encourage new shoot growth, or in midsummer if you want to discourage suckering.

## Mechanical Support

Weak limbs can sometimes be propped or held together with mechanical supports such as braces or cables. These supports can alleviate the stress on a weak branch or leader. Installing support in a large tree is not a do-it-yourself job. You may be able

to install a cable in a smaller ornamental tree, though. Most of the tools and equipment you will need are available at the local hardware store. A weak limb can also be supported by a brace, a crutch between the ground and the branch. It's important to place the brace correctly and attach it to the tree properly.

Improperly installed cables and braces can do more harm than good to a tree. If a wire or other support is wrapped too

**Cabling is one way to maintain an old tree that threatens to break apart.**

**Sometimes a special tree requires special treatment. At around 90 years old, this Caucasian wingnut (*Pterocarya fraxinifolia*), a cherished veteran at Brooklyn Botanic Garden, receives a bit of mechanical support to keep a large scaffold limb from breaking under its own weight.**

tightly around a branch, the wire can dig into live wood as the tree grows, girdling it and, in effect, strangling the tree. The Tree Care Industry Association (TCIA) has published standards on how to install cables and bracing. (See page 114 for a Web link.) The eminent tree biologist Alex Shigo recommends that cabling, bracing, and other practices that can wound the tree not be done during spring growth or at leaf fall in autumn.

# Dying and Dead Trees

The death of a tree, especially one that has sentimental value, can be traumatic, whether it dies suddenly as a result of a natural disaster like a hurricane, fire, or ice storm; over a few months after an infestation by deadly insects or pathogens; or over a long period simply from old age, as it runs out of energy or falls apart. We can help slow the spread of diseases and pests and improve the health and survival chances of more trees by planting diverse species and providing consistent and thoughtful care. We can also prolong the lives of trees by calling in an arborist at the first sign of trouble. Sadly, many arborists report that most calls for help come when a tree is already in major decline or deceased, when there are few options other than removing the tree. To prolong the life of your tree, get help before it reaches terminal decline.

Even when we care for trees well and prune and mulch them properly, we are helpless when a pandemic or natural disaster occurs. New diseases and pest infestations travel rapidly around the world in ships' cargo holds, planes' bellies, and in passengers' bags from spots where trees have evolved a natural resistance to them to areas where trees have never been exposed to them and are extremely vulnerable. These types of problems can quickly devastate large plantings of mature trees. Neighborhoods and towns hit by natural disasters like floods or outbreaks of deadly insects like the recently arrived emerald ash borer or pathogens like Dutch elm disease will not be able to easily replace the shade and beauty their mature trees provided for decades.

The demise of a tree from less dramatic causes can be a very slow process. Some trees may look as if they are at death's door for years. Over that time the balance of

**How do you tell whether a tree is dead? Some indications are missing bark, lack of foliage, and brittle wood. If a tree fails to leaf out for a whole season, it's most likely dead.**

living and dead tissue in a tree gradually shifts; the living part becomes smaller and smaller until it can no longer support the tree. As the roots and stem of large dead trees decay, they sooner or later fail or break apart. Dead and dying trees pose safety issues, and depending on their proximity to people, structures, and other plants, they may need to be removed.

Unfortunately, people often remove trees that have not reached this point in their life cycle. They cut down healthy, live trees to clear lots for development, when they feel that a tree has become too big or too messy, or because they want to change the landscape. Some communities have enacted laws that limit a homeowner's right to remove trees, even on private property. Zoning has improved in many communities to take into account the value of green spaces.

Most arborists I know do not object to removing a live tree for sound reasons but will refuse jobs when the rationale does not make sense. A lot of fly-by-night "tree surgeons" will happily remove any tree. But client beware: Not only is the removal of a large tree expensive, when done improperly it can result in damage to property and nearby plants.

## Lazarus Trees and Stump Sprouts

A dying tree can sometimes go on to have a second life. For example, in stands of old orchard trees that look very close to death, I've often seen new stems suckering up

from a tree's base, forming a "Lazarus tree." Not all species will do this, but some trees like cherries, crabapples, lindens, and willows sometimes break apart, then sucker out new sprouts from the roots or even from a stump after the tree has been cut down. In forestry terms this a stump sprout. These shoots can be pruned and trained into a new tree.

**Sometimes a new tree can sprout from the base of a decaying one, as occurred with this Sargent cherry, *Prunus sargentii*.**

You don't have to remove a tree just because parts of it are no longer alive. A dead or dying tree is a boon to wildlife and can become an asset to your garden, provided there's no danger to people or property. A woodpecker has been using this dead sycamore branch to stash acorns.

## Habitat Trees

Long after they die, trees can play an important role in the environment as habitat for thousands of other living organisms. In the forest, standing dead trees, known as snags, become refuges and sources of food for birds, mammals, reptiles, insects, and other plants and fungi. A dead or dying tree that does not pose a safety threat can make a good habitat tree for your garden and will encourage more wildlife to come into your yard. Remove some of the top of the tree to make it safer, but leave the trunk and some branches. Trees with wood that resists rot are better candidates for habitat trees than fast-decaying trees like willows, poplars, cherries, or pines. White oak, cedar, and locust actually produce chemicals that resist rot and can stand for many years. Beetles, salamanders, and tree frogs all use loose bark as shelter, and barred owls, squirrels, opossums, and many other creatures will nest in the trees' cavities. These miniature ecosystems are ideal places to observe and show children nature at work. For the more adventurous, decaying trees and logs bring to life many species of fungi and insects. You just have to get in close and take a look.

## Nurse Logs

Nurse logs, sometimes called "mother stumps," are fallen branches and trunks that remain on the forest floor—or in the backyard—helping the tree's biomass return to the soil where it rightfully belongs. Nurse logs, like habitat trees, have long productive afterlives as they provide the soil with nutrients and are home to beneficial microorganisms. They are also ideal places in the forest for new seedlings to get started. In a garden bed, a well-placed log or interestingly formed branch can provide visual interest and support other plants while improving the soil. Nurse logs can

**As it slowly decays and is incorporated back into the soil, a dead branch or tree trunk provides food and shelter for insects, fungi, and other organisms.**

also give your garden a more natural feel. Some arborists even sell nurse logs from the trees they remove. This is a great way to make use of wood that might otherwise end up in a landfill.

## Green Waste and Timber From Urban Trees

A large or even medium-sized tree can have a surprising amount of wood. That wood should not end up in a landfill. Over 200 million cubic yards of green waste—everything from lawn clippings and leaves to logs and branches—are generated in urban areas each year. This green waste is costly for communities to dispose of, and most of it can and should instead be put to good use.

Tree-service companies and landscaping contractors often use wood chippers to chip branches and logs from pruning and removal jobs. Wood chips are a great mulch to use around trees or in garden beds. The can also be composted and used to amend soil. Some cities now offer separate leaf and wood collections and provide opportunities for residents to pick up free compost and wood chips. If you plan to do a lot of pruning or remove a small tree, consider renting a wood chipper from a local tool-rental business. Depending on the size of the chipper, you can feed it limbs up to six inches in diameter. Be careful, though: Brush chippers are dangerous. Get a lesson first, keep children away, and make sure you wear eye and ear protection. Chipping can save you lots of time and effort and will provide you with mulch to put back into the garden.

Burning large pieces of wood in an open fireplace is quite popular, but it puts lots of carbon back into the air. There are, however, wood-burning stoves available that burn cleaner and which are more efficient at heating your home.

Another environmentally friendly way to deal with large pieces of sound wood is to have it milled into lumber. A small but growing number of tree services have portable band-saw mills that they can tow right to a job site. Tree trunks that would otherwise end up in a landfill are milled into boards, which can either be sold or used by the homeowner. In his book *Harvesting Urban Timber,* Sam Sherrill explains that if we milled the hardwood trees that we currently remove from cities every year, we could save thousands of forest trees that are cut down for timber.

## Stump Removal

So you had that tree removed, and now you've got a big stump. Stumps take up a lot of precious space in your yard or garden beds and can even sprout—and if the tree was a hardwood, it could stick around for a long time. Many tree services will grind down stumps using machines that reach 12 to 18 inches below the surface. Stump grinding can be quite expensive, though. I've sped up the rotting of stumps by drilling holes into the top and then inoculating them with fertilizer, which promotes decay. Other options include incorporating the stump into your garden design, turning it into a rustic garden seat, and letting it decay at its own pace as a habitat for fungi and other organisms.

**Removing a stump can be quite costly. If you don't mind the space it occupies, leave the stump to decay on its own and turn into habitat.**

# Choosing Trees

Whenever possible, plant trees in groves, combining species with similar moisture and soil requirements. Growing trees in a group mimics how they grow in nature and tends to result in trees that are healthier and easier to care for. Individual trees in a group will have a smaller canopy than open-grown trees, but they will also develop fewer heavy (and potentially hazardous) lateral limbs.

## A Word on Native and Invasive Trees

A native tree is generally understood to be one that has not been introduced by people either intentionally or by accident. Trees that are native to a certain region are usually well suited to the climate, soil type, rainfall, and other environmental conditions because they have evolved with the local ecosystem for many generations. They tend to be well adapted to their home region and will do well in a yard provided that they are planted in conditions that resemble their natural habitats. They are more resistant to the insects and diseases that are also native to your area and rarely require applications of fertilizers or pesticides. Native plants also often attract the beneficial insects that prey upon pests: According to the National Wildlife Federation, they provide food and shelter for 10 to 15 times more species of birds, butterflies, and other local wildlife than nonnative plants. The inconspicuous flowers of North American black gum or black tupelo (*Nyssa sylvatica*), for example, are more attractive to native short-tongued bees than to nonnative bees. The blue fruit is consumed by bears, foxes, raccoons, and many birds, such as migrating robins.

**For long-term success, pick trees that are adapted to the growing conditions in your yard. This beautiful lacebark pine (*Pinus bungeana*) grows best in full sun and moist, well-drained soils.**

A few nonnative trees that are commonly planted in gardens have escaped cultivation, invading wild areas and degrading them by displacing other plants and the wildlife that depends on them. If you are unsure whether a tree may be problematic in your area, check with your local invasive pest plant council before acquiring it.

## A Note on Nomenclature

Establishing a tree's identity can be confusing. For example, the common names red maple, scarlet maple, and swamp maple all refer to the same tree, known in the botanical world as *Acer rubrum*. The ponderosa pine (*Pinus ponderosa*) is also called western yellow pine and blackjack pine. And on it goes. Most tree species have more than one common name, but luckily they all have just one botanical name, recognizable to anyone in the world. A species' name has two parts: The first is the genus to which the plant belongs. Botanists have grouped together species that share a number of significant features into a genus. The members of the genus *Acer*, for example, all produce distinctive winged fruit called samaras; their young shoots in spring are red; they flower early; they are generally deciduous; and their leaves are produced in pairs opposite each other. Next in a species

name comes the specific epithet, for example, *rubrum* (meaning red), which usually tells something about the species that sets it apart from others in its genus. If a plant is a cultivar of a species propagated for specific desirable characteristics of flower, color, habit, size, variegation, or fruit color or flavor, it will have an additional name in single quotes. *Acer rubrum* 'Schlesingeri' has deep red, wavy-edged leaves in fall, while *A. rubrum* 'Scanlon' has a compact, upright shape and deep

**Be sure to read the plant label to avoid surprises. The cultivar name 'Pendulum' of this katsura tree (*Cercidiphyllum japonicum* var. *magnificum* 'Pendulum') indicates that it is a weeping form.**

**Consider other trees already growing in the vicinity when you pick a tree, and choose one that complements their sizes, colors, and shapes.**

red to purple leaves in fall. As new plant species are discovered and new evidence of evolutionary relationships is provided by molecular studies, botanists often find previously unknown plant relationships, so plant names occasionally change.

## Tree Selection Tips

- Know the mature size of any tree you are planting. If you already have a canopy of large trees in your yard, choose understory trees to plant beneath them.

- Consider aesthetics: Select trees with foliage and flower colors that complement those of your existing trees.

- Avoid monoculture: Combine different species to curb the spread of diseases and insects.

- Determine how much shade is cast by existing trees and whether a potential new tree can thrive with the amount of available light.

- Avoid trees with lots of large, woody surface roots like maples (*Acer* species), if you want to combine several trees.

- Refer to the site checklist, page 31, to determine the requirements of your tree-planting site.

# List of Trees

## SMALL TO MEDIUM-SIZED TREES

| | HARDINESS ZONE AND REGIONS | SIZE | SOIL REQUIREMENTS |
|---|---|---|---|
| *Acer griseum* | 5; NE, MW | 25' | moist, well-drained soils |
| *Acer × rotundilobum** | 7–9; SE | 20–25' | wet soils |
| *Amelanchier arborea** | 3–9; NE, SE | 15–25' | moist, well-drained, acidic soils |
| *Chionanthus retusus** | 5–8; NE, SE, MW | 20–30' | extremely adaptable |
| *Cornus kousa** | 5; NE, SE, MW | 35' | moist, well-drained, acidic soils |
| *Halesia tetraptera** | 4–9; NE, SE, MW, NW | 30–40' | moist, well-drained, acidic soils |
| *Koelreuteria paniculata* | 5; all but NW | 35' | adaptable to dry or poor soils |
| *Magnolia virginiana** | 5–9; NE, SE | 10–30' | adaptable to wet, acidic soils |
| *Ostrya virginiana** | 3–9; NE, SE | 25–40' | moist, well-drained, slightly acidic soils |
| *Pinus koraiensis* | 4–7; NE | 30–40' | adaptable to many soils |
| *Pistacia chinensis* | 6–9; Cal., SW | 30–35' | drought tolerant; very adaptable to soils |
| *Stewartia pseudocamellia** | 5–7; NE, SE, MW, NW | 20–40' | moist, acidic soils |

## MEDIUM-SIZED TO LARGE TREES

| | | | |
|---|---|---|---|
| *Acer rubrum* | 3–9; NE, SE, MW, NW | 40–60' | moist to wet, acidic soils |
| *Aesculus × carnea* | 4–7; NE, SE, MW, NW | 60–70' | well-drained soils; pH adaptable |
| *Betula lenta* | 3–7; NE, MW | 40–50' | moist, well-drained acidic soils |
| *Betula nigra* | 3–9; NE, SE, MW, NW | 40–70' | wet to well-drained fertile, acidic soils |
| *Carpinus betulus** | 5–7; NE, MW | 40' | wide range of well-drained soils |
| *Cercidiphyllum japonicum* | 4–8; NE, MW, SE | 40–60' | moist, acidic soils |
| *Cinnamomum camphora** | 9–11; SE | 40–60' | acidic sandy or clay loam soils; tolerates dry conditions |
| *Cupressus arizonica* | 7–9; SW | 40–60' | well-drained soils; adapted to dry conditions |
| *Ginkgo biloba* | 4–8; NE, SE, MW, NW, Cal. | 50–80' | very adaptable to soils |
| *Fagus sylvatica* | 4–7; NE | 50–70' | moist, well-drained acidic soils |
| *Gleditsia triacanthos* | 4–9; NE, SE, MW | 30–70' | very adaptable |
| *Liquidambar styraciflua* | 5–9; NE, SE, MW | 60–75' | moist, slightly acidic soils |

| | HARDINESS ZONE AND REGIONS | SIZE | SOIL REQUIREMENTS |
|---|---|---|---|
| *Nyssa sylvatica** | 4–9; NE, SE, MW | 40–50' | moist to wet; well-drained, acidic soils of pH 5.5–6.5 |
| *Oxydendrum arboreum** | 5–9; NE, SE, MW | 30–40' | moist, well-drained, slightly acidic soils |
| *Picea orientalis** | 4–7; NE, MW | 50–60' | tolerates poor soils |
| *Pinus bungeana** | 4–7; NE | 40–80' | well-drained soils; high-pH adaptable |
| *Sophora japonica* | 4–7; NE | 50–75' | well-drained soils; heat and drought tolerant |

## LARGE TREES

| | HARDINESS ZONE AND REGIONS | SIZE | SOIL REQUIREMENTS |
|---|---|---|---|
| *Abies nordmanniana* | 4–6; NE | 60–100' | moist, well-drained acidic soils |
| *Acer saccharum* | 4–8; NE | 60–100' | moist, well-drained fertile soils, pH adaptable |
| *Celtis laevigata* | 5–9; SE, NE | 60–80' | adaptable to urban conditions; tolerates compacted and wet soils |
| *Magnolia grandiflora** | 6–9; SE | 60–100' | rich, well-drained, acidic soils |
| *Metasequoia glyptostroboides* | 4–8; NE, SE, MW, NW | 70–100' | moist, well-drained, slightly acidic soils |
| *Pinus ponderosa* | 3–6; NW, SW | 60–100' | well-drained, loamy soils, tolerates high pH, salt, drought |
| *Platanus racemosa* | 7–9; Cal. | 70–90' | wet to moist, rich soils |
| *Pseudolarix amabilis* | 4–7; NE, SE, MW | 50–80' | moist, well-drained, rich soils |
| *Quercus bicolor* | 4–8; NE, SE, MW | 50–80' | moist to somewhat wet, acidic soils |
| *Quercus coccinea* | 4–9; NE, SE | 60–100' | dry, sandy soils |
| *Quercus shumardii* | 5–9; NE, SE, MW | 50–80' | drought tolerant; acidic to alkaline soils |
| *Quercus virginiana* | 7–10; SE, SW | 40–80' | tolerates moist and compacted soils |
| *Taxodium distichum* | 4–11; NE, SE, MW | 50–80' | adaptable to wet, dry, and well-drained, acidic soils |
| *Tilia tomentosa* | 4–7; NE | 50–70' | moist, well-drained fertile soils; pH adaptable |
| *Ulmus alata* | 5–9; NE, SE, MW | 60–80' | very adaptable |
| *Zelkova serrata* | 4–8; NE, SE, MW, NW, Cal. | 50–80' | moist soils; drought tolerant once established |

*These trees are shade tolerant.*

# Tree Health Care

Trees are generally able to defend themselves to some extent at every stage of their lives. They produce many types of chemical compounds as protection against harmful fungi, herbivores, and even other plants. These compounds can be found in most parts of the tree, and some can even be emitted into the air (think of the smell of pines or eucalyptus trees). Some trees may put as much as 15 percent of their energy resources toward chemical defenses, which helps explain why stressed trees, whose energy resources are depleted, are more prone to attack and damage.

## Preventive Care

Since healthy trees are much better at fending off a pest or disease attack than stressed trees, your best approach is to create a tree-friendly environment and be vigilant:

- Keep trees watered and mulched as needed.
- Protect the tree's root zone and soil from compaction and contamination.
- Avoid overpruning and topping.
- Monitor trees during the growing season for key pests in your area.
- Check with your state cooperative extension for updates on pest problems and resistant tree species or cultivars.
- Plant insect and disease-resistant species and cultivars when there is an insect or disease problem in your area.

In addition, try to monitor your trees' health by looking for signs of pests or diseases and other changes and abnormalities, such as stem or twig dieback, excessive deadwood, wilting, discoloration of leaves, early fall color, and early leaf drop. Periodically check for spots or feeding damage on the leaves and for fungal growth on the trunk, branches, or leaves. Take note of loose or dropped bark, suckering at the base of the tree, or water sprouts on the branches.

If a problem is identified early, a tree can most likely be treated using nontoxic methods. Local public gardens and state cooperative extension services are great resources. They will help you identify insects and plant diseases and keep you updated on invasive pests that may be heading toward your area.

Many landscape and tree services offer maintenance packages that can do the work for you. Promoting a holistic approach to tree care, integrated pest management (IPM) and preventive health care (PHC) have emerged as industry standards in recent years. Integrated pest manage-

**Volcano mulching is a bad practice that is regrettably widespread. Apply mulch just a few inches deep and keep it well away from the trunk.**

ment entails identifying pests and managing them with the least invasive strategy possible. Preventive health care is aimed at keeping trees strong and healthy so that they will be better able to defend themselves if there is an infestation. A PHC company will visit your property up to several times a month in the growing season to survey plants for insects and diseases and other problems.

A good tree service will monitor the health of your trees with regular inspections. It will inform you about any pests or diseases found and the effect they will have on the trees and suggest treatment options. Avoid companies that offer to douse your trees with broad-spectrum pesticides because "it's the time of year to spray." Aside from their effects on you, your children, pets, and the environment at large, broad-spectrum pesticides kill both bad insects and beneficial ones. Many broad-spectrum pesticides are used more to line the pockets of unscrupulous tree services than to help trees.

## Boosting Tree Health With Compost

Amending the soil with compost is an age-old gardening practice that helps enrich the soil with organic matter teeming with beneficial organisms. As the compost blends into the soil bacteria, fungi, protozoa, and beneficial nematodes multiply and spread into the surrounding soil. The movement of the organisms opens up the pore spaces, improving aeration and alleviating compaction over time. The microorganisms also increase the amount of nutrients available to plants.

While compost is a wonderful soil amendment for trees, it cannot be worked into the soil without damaging the roots of established trees. That's where compost tea comes in. Compost tea is made by steeping finished compost for a number of days in water, then spraying plant foliage with the nutrient-rich water or drenching the soil around plants. Some commercially available compost-brewing kits have an aeration system that adds air into the water as the tea steeps, which keeps it from going anaerobic (or smelly). When you are making compost tea at home, mix one gallon of brewed compost tea with 10 to 15 gallons of water and drench the root zones of your trees. You can also customize the tea by adding nutrient-rich materials such as sea kelp, humus, or even molasses to help feed and build up microorganisms. Another option is hiring a professional arborist who specializes in compost tea and soil care, a relatively recent field of study. The arborist will examine the soil biology and then custom-brew a tea formulated for your soil's needs. No matter how sophisticated your approach, I find that compost tea is an excellent and environmentally sound way to improve the quality of landscape soil and boost the long-term health of your trees.

## Helping Trees Cope With Extreme Weather

Trees inadequately cared for during spring and summer droughts or before potentially lethal winter storms may fall victim to extreme weather. To help trees through drought, irrigation is key. If your area experiences two to three weeks with little or no rain, consider supplemental watering, even for mature trees. Place a sprinkler or a hose at the base of these trees for two hours or so once a week during a drought. Be sure to set your watering equipment up in such a way that the stream of water doesn't wash away mulch and soil, exposing roots. It's even more important to water younger trees because they have a less developed root system. Signs that a tree needs water include wilting, browning of leaves, and most drastically, premature leaf fall. Watering is especially important if the dry spell occurs toward the end of the growing season, when trees are entering their dormant period. If plants don't take up

**It may look picturesque, but a heavy load of snow adds considerable weight to branches and should be removed. If you live in an area with lots of snow, consider propping up lower limbs.**

enough water during the growing season, the new growth that they have put on can dry out and die during the winter. This "tip dieback" will be visible the following spring, and it can be fatal for a tree.

Proper pruning will help trees survive winter storms, which can coat them with a heavy layer of snow or ice. In areas where heavy snowfall and ice storms are common, prop up the lower branches of trees and knock the snow off branches after heavy snowfalls. Stay away from trees that are heavily coated with ice—the weight of the ice may bring limbs crashing down.

## Protecting Trees Against Pests and Diseases

As people and goods move freely around the globe, pests and pathogens are hitching rides and moving into new areas. This is true for pests and pathogens that infect us, like West Nile virus, hepatitis, and SARS, and also applies to major tree pests and diseases. Recently introduced by accident in shipping materials and the like, insects such as Asian longhorned beetle, emerald ash borer, and hemlock woolly adelgid have already killed millions of trees and threaten many more. The gypsy moth has been devastating North American forests for over a century and shows little sign of slowing down. Entomologists aren't the only ones keeping busy though; plant pathologists are also seeing a host of new diseases. George Hudler of Cornell University recently identified a microbe that has been killing European beech trees in the Northeast for the past 30 years. Sudden oak death is claiming the lives of landscape

A recently introduced pest, the emerald ash borer is wreaking havoc on ash trees in the Midwest. Above is the adult beetle, which is only about half an inch long.

The one-inch-long Asian longhorned beetle is threatening many deciduous tree species in the Northeast. To contain the spread of the beetle, affected trees and susceptible host trees in the vicinity are being removed.

and forest trees in large numbers in California. Meanwhile, other pathogens that have been causing devastation for decades, like those responsible for Dutch elm disease and chestnut blight, have steadily spread westward to infect trees in new territories.

Ultimately, there may be little gardeners can do to save trees from infestation. Some pests, such as the emerald ash borer, currently attacking ash trees in the Midwest, seem to move too quickly to be contained. In cases like this, drastic measures must be taken: A tree found to be infested with the pest is automatically removed by order of the U.S. Department of Agriculture. The wood is chipped and then burned. Furthermore, other ash trees nearby may also be removed to control the insects' movement. While it is sad to lose a tree, at this time removal is the only known control for some pests.

To contain the spread of Asian longhorned beetle, insecticides have been used as a preventative. Many arborists believe that repeated treatment with the injectable insecticide may actually do more harm than good to healthy trees by damaging their vascular system. The rapid spread of some pests and pathogens leaves little time to answer such important questions before control measures must be taken.

Many deadly insects and diseases are pretty resilient and are probably here to stay. Over time, nature itself will more than likely play the biggest role in controlling outbreaks and finding a dynamic equilibrium between the pest and its host.

# The Language of Tree Care

**Apical dominance** The suppression by a stem's terminal bud of lateral bud growth.

**Branch bark ridge** A ridge of bark, often visible as a dark line, that starts in the branch union and extends onto the trunk.

**Branch collar** A thickened area around the base of a branch where branch and stem tissues meet.

**Branch union** The area where the trunk and branch meet.

**Cambium zone** A very thin layer of meristematic cells found just below the bark in a tree's stem and roots that makes secondary phloem on the outside and secondary xylem on the inside. It is responsible for secondary growth, which increases a tree's girth. The cambium zone also responds to structural needs by adding more xylem (wood) to weaker areas of the stem or roots.

**Compartmentalization** The process by which a tree reacts when wounded by forming both physical and chem-

**Removing one of two codominant stems is an important pruning task, best done when the tree is young. Codominant stems make for weak branch unions that can become hazardous on large branches.**

ical boundaries within its stem and woody roots that resist the spread of infection. This is the tree's defense from decay. As a tree compartmentalizes infected wood, its storage space for energy reserves is reduced.

**Drip line** The outermost branch tips, or perimeter of a tree's canopy, from which rainwater drips to the ground. The drip line was formerly thought to be the outer reaches of the root system, but it is now known that in many species the roots can grow well beyond that area.

**Dynamic mass** All the parts of the tree containing living parenchyma cells—thin-walled cells essential in photosynthesis and food storage.

**Lateral bud** A vegetative bud on the side of a stem. Some lateral buds may grow to become new branches.

**Meristem** Plant tissue that consists of rapidly dividing undefined cells, found in root tips, buds, cambium, and cork cambium.

**Mycorrhiza, -ae** (mycor = fungus, rhiza = root) An association between beneficial fungi and nonwoody roots of a plant that helps the plant with the absorption of water, phosphates, and other soil elements. Most trees need this symbiotic association with mycorrhizal fungi to remain healthy. Soil compaction, drought, overfertilization, and fungicides can harm mycorrhizal fungi.

**Phloem** Vascular tissue lying between the cambium zone and the bark. The phloem moves food and growth regulators up or down the tree.

**Photosynthesis** The process by which plants make sugar. It requires chlorophyll (the green pigment in leaves), solar energy, carbon dioxide, and water.

**Phototropism** Growth that is determined by the direction of sunlight.

In this cross-section view, the dark area in the wood shows compartmentalization: After the branch was removed, the tree formed a chemical barrier to contain the spread of infection entering through the open wound.

**The white coating on these tree roots indicates the presence of root fungi that form a mutually beneficial relationship with tree roots, called mycorrhizae.**

Respiration The process by which plants and animals convert the energy stored in carbohydrates to fuel metabolic processes and growth.

Rhizosphere The zone about one millimeter in width around a tree's absorbing roots where there is mycorrhizal interface with the soil. This rhizosphere and surrounding soils is a very dynamic place where soil organisms compete for food, water, and space.

Static mass As the cells of the inner wood of a tree die, they become static (no longer living). Yet this wood can still be load bearing as part of the heartwood or other forms of protection wood.

Terminal bud The bud at tip of a shoot or twig where primary growth takes place on the stem.

Transpiration A plant's loss of water in the form of vapor through stomates—small pores on the underside of leaves—as well as through stems, flowers, and fruit.

Woundwood Riblike wood that grows around a wounded area of a tree's stem and sometimes roots. After a tree is wounded, say, by a pruning cut, callus tissue first forms; eventually the callus cells become more lignified, forming woundwood. This very tough woody tissue helps give the tree more structural support.

Xylem Conducting tissue inside the cambium zone by which water and minerals move up the tree. Xylem tissue eventually becomes lignified, or woody.

# USDA Hardiness Zone Map

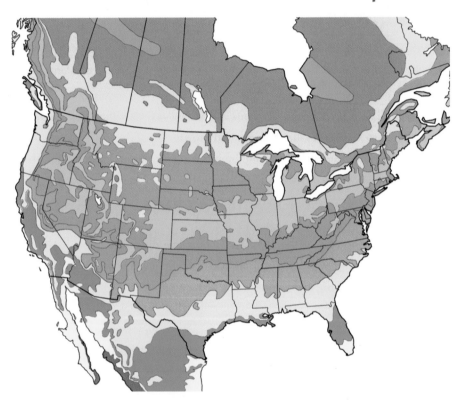

## Zones and Minimum Winter Temperatures (°F.)

Zone 1  below −50°

Zone 2  −50° to −40°

Zone 3  −40° to −30°

Zone 4  −30° to −20°

Zone 5  −20° to 10°

Zone 6  −10° to 0°

Zone 7  0° to 10°

Zone 8  10° to 20°

Zone 9  20° to 30°

Zone 10  30° to 40°

Zone 11  above 40°

# Nursery and Tool Sources

## NURSERIES

American Forests Historic Tree Nursery
P.O. Box 2000
Washington, DC 20013
202-737-1944
www.historictrees.org/store.html

Buckeye Nursery
P.O. Box 450
Perry, FL 32347
800-838-2218
www.buckeyenursery.com

Fairweather Gardens
P.O. Box 330
Greenwich, NJ 08323
856-451-6261
www.fairweathergardens.com

Forestfarm
990 Tetherow Road
Williams, OR 97544
541-846-7269
www.forestfarm.com

Green Tree Nursery
23979 Lake Road
La Grange, CA 95327
800-350-4414
www.greentreenursery.com

Nature Hills Nursery
3334 North 88th Plaza
Omaha, NB 68134
402-934-8116
www.naturehills.com

Rosedale Nurseries
51 Saw Mill River Road
Hawthorne, NY 10532
914-769-1300
www.rosedalenurseries.com

Swanson's Nursery
9701 15th Avenue N.W.
Seattle, WA 98117
www.swansonsnursery.com

Woodlanders
1128 Colleton Avenue
Aiken, SC 29801
803-648-7522
www.woodlanders.net

## TOOL SUPPLIERS

American Arborist Supplies
882 South Matlack Street, Unit A
West Chester, PA 19382
800-441-8381
www.arborist.com

A.M. Leonard
421 Fox Drive, P.O. Box 816
Piqua, OH 45356
800-543-8955
www.amleo.com

Fresco Arborist Supplies
13705 26th Ave. N., Suite 116
Plymouth, MN 55441
866-353-3326
www.frescoarborist.com

Stone Lantern
P.O. Box 70
Passumpsic, VT 05861
800-776-1167
www.stonelantern.com

WesSpur Tree Equipment
1680 Baker Creek Place
Bellingham, WA 98226
800-268-2141
www.wesspur.com

# For More Information

**BOOKS ABOUT TREE CARE**

*Cass Turnbull's Guide to Pruning*
By Cass Turnbull
Sasquatch Books, 2006

*The Compost Tea Brewing Manual*
By Elaine Ingham
Soil Foodweb, Inc., 1999

*Evaluating Tree Defects*
By Ed Hayes
Safetrees, LLC, 2001

*IPM for Gardeners*
By Raymond Cloyd, Philip Nixon, and
Nancy Pataky
Timber Press, 2004

*Manual of Woody Landscape Plants*
By Michael A. Dirr
Stipes Publishing, 1998

*Oak: The Frame of Civilization*
By William Bryant Logan
WW. Norton & Co., 2005

*Once Upon a Tree: Life From Treetop to
Root Tips*
By James Nardi
Iowa State University Press, 1993

*Recommended Urban Trees: Site Assessment
and Tree Selection for Stress Tolerance*
By Urban Horticulture Institute
Cornell University, 2003

*Trees: Their Natural History*
By Peter Thomas
Cambridge University Press, 2001

*Tree Pruning: A Worldwide Photo Guide*
By Alex L. Shigo
Shigo and Trees Associates, 1989

*Trees of North America: A Field Guide
to the Major Native and Introduced Species
North of Mexico*
Golden Guides From St. Martin's Press,
2001

**WEBSITES ABOUT TREE CARE**

www.asca-consultants.org
American Society of Consulting Arborists;
referral directory for arborists and other
information

www.isa-arbor.com
International Society of Arboriculture;
promoting research, technology, and
professional practice of arboriculture

www.treesaregood.com
Trees Are Good; consumer site of ISA
offering tree-care information

www.soilfoodweb.com
Soil Foodweb, Inc.; soil biology, with
emphasis on use of compost tea

www.natlarb.com
Tree Care Industry Association; tree care
information, resources for consumers and
tree care professionals

www.csrees.usda.gov/extension
USDA Cooperative State Research, Education
and Extension Service; links to state and
county cooperative extensions in the U.S.

# Contributors

Christopher Roddick is an ISA-certified staff arborist at Brooklyn Botanic Garden. Formerly the head arborist at Scott Arboretum, in Swarthmore, Pennsylvania, he is currently a tree consultant and instructor specializing in mature tree preservation, pruning, and tree diagnostics. He has climbed, pruned, and cared for trees all over the U.S. for more than 20 years and has also been on two expeditions to French Guyana doing tree canopy research.

Beth Hanson is former managing editor of Brooklyn Botanic Garden's handbook series and editor of nine handbooks, including *The Best Apples to Buy and Grow* (2005), *Designing an Herb Garden* (2004), *Natural Disease Control* (2000), *Chile Peppers* (1999), and *Easy Compost* (1997). She also contributed to *The Brooklyn Botanic Garden Gardener's Desk Reference* (1998). She lives outside New York City and writes about gardening, health, and the environment for various publications.

## Illustrations

Katherine Dana

Illustrations on page 53 are based on drawings by **Steven K-M. Tim** that originally appeared in *The Brooklyn Botanic Garden's Gardener's Desk Reference* (1998).

## Photos

Elizabeth Ennis cover, pages 20, 37, 40, 48

Jerry Pavia pages 2, 17, 21, 27, 29, 47, 68, 71, 98, 100

David Cavagnaro pages 5, 8, 15 both, 62, 72, 80, 82, 92, 95

Neil Soderstrom pages 6, 9, 10, 11, 12, 14 both, 18, 23, 24, 25, 26, 30, 32 (Hollandia Nursery & Garden Center, Bethel, CT), 34, 36, 39, 42 both, 43, 44 both, 45, 54 all, 55, 56, 63, 64, 65, 76 both, 79, 83, 86, 90, 91, 96, 97, 107, 109, 110, 111, 113

Christopher Roddick pages 35, 59 both, 66, 84, 85, 94, 101, 105

Beth Hanson pages 58, 73, 77

David Cappaert, www.insectimages.org page 108

USDA APHIS Archives, USDA APHIS, www.insectimages.org page 108

Special thanks go to **Alec Baxt**, staff arborist at Brooklyn Botanic Garden, for reviewing the text.

# Index

# More Information on Responsible Gardening

Invasive plants are one of the greatest threats to native plants and animals in North America, and about half of the worst species currently degrading natural habitats from coast to coast were introduced intentionally, for horticultural use. In *Native Alternatives to Invasive Plants,* plant professionals and home gardeners alike will discover hundreds of spectacular native plants for every region, specially chosen as alternatives to the invasive species that are threatening the continent's remaining wild landscapes. The beautiful wildflowers, shrubs, and trees profiled in this double-length handbook are organized by plant type for easy reference, with one to four native alternatives recommended for every invasive plant. "Attributes at a Glance" boxes highlight each plant's most attractive features, including its appeal to butterflies, birds, and other wildlife.

## Ordering Books From Brooklyn Botanic Garden

World renowned for pioneering gardening information, Brooklyn Botanic Garden's award-winning guides provide practical advice for gardeners in every region of North America.

Join Brooklyn Botanic Garden as an annual Subscriber Member and receive three gardening handbooks, delivered directly to you, each year. Other benefits include free admission to many public gardens across the country, plus three issues of *Plants & Gardens News, Members News,* and our guide to courses and public programs.

For additional information about Brooklyn Botanic Garden, including other membership packages, call 718-623-7210 or visit our website at www.bbg.org. To order other fine titles published by BBG, call 718-623-7286 or shop in our online store at http://shop.bbg.org.